No Small Change

Succeeding in Canada's New Economy

Dian Cohen
and Guy Stanley

Canadian Cataloguing in Publication Data

Cohen, Dian
  No small change: succeeding in Canada's new economy

Includes index.
ISBN 0-7715-9179-9

1. Canada – Economic conditions – 1991- 2. Industrial productivity – Canada. I. Stanley, Guy II. Title.

HC115.C65   1993   330.971'0647   C92-094310-1

Macmillan Canada wishes to thank the Canada Council for supporting its publishing program.

Macmillian Canada
A Division of Canada Publishing Corporation
Toronto, Canada

Phoenix Antique is certified by Environmental Choice^M to contain 50% recycled paper including 10% post-consumer fibre.
M – Official mark of Environment Canada

1   2   3   4   5   FP   97   96   95   94   93

Printed in Canada

For Lisa, Nina, Tamara,
Lance, Paul and Gaby

Find some things you love to do,
then spend the rest of your life doing them.
D.C.

Ilona, Arthur and David and our mothers,
Faith, Susan and Eliza.

G.S.

Contents

Acknowledgements

To LANSING LAMONT and the Rockfeller and Donner Foundations for a stimulating year at the Americas Society in New York; to the managers and stakeholders of the companies and associations I am privileged to serve, every one of you, colleagues and strangers alike who respond so generously with your time whenever I phone, the viewers of CTV and Canada AM, the listeners of CJRT-Open College, Ryerson, Adriana Escobar, my children and their father, all for sharing your insights and contributing vastly to my education; to Jane Sanderson, Cheryl Kalau, John Valenteyn, Pat Billing, Terri Foxman, and Rosa Harris-Adler, for the best administrative, communications and organizational help available; to Tib Beament and Ping Gee for inspirational craftsmanship; to Ron Besse, Denise Schon, Philippa Campsie, Kirsten Hanson and Jennifer Glossop for support from beginning to end; to my multi-talented friend and co-author, Guy Stanley, from whom we should all take lessons in understanding and adapting to change; and to Nickolas Murray, whose insistence on independent thinking is often disquieting, but always fun.

–D.C.

To friends and colleagues: at HEC, especially Andre Poirier, Francois Leroux and Dennis Chaput, who created the opportunity, to Gunnar Sletmo for his insight on product cycles and Martyne Cimon for keeping track, and to Gilles Gauthier, for cherished illusions; at the Americas Society, especially Stephen Blank and Susan Sorrell for unfailing encouragement and support, and to Leressa Crockett for insights into the way things work as well as her patience; to students in my seminars on North American free trade for wanting to know more, to Mme Deschenes for helping me organize; to clients, whose problems shed so much light on the way things are; to the on-line data base providers, especially InfoGlobe, InfoMart, Dow Jones, Dialog, Newsnet and Compuserve. And above all to Dian Cohen, whose special gifts delight her associates, friends and fans.

–G.S.

Preface

THIS BOOK IS about the new economy and the Canadians who are leading the way. It's designed to help you understand and benefit from the changes going on. It's not a book about economics, although there's a smattering of economics here and there. It's a book about change—the impact of technological changes in the last quarter of the twentieth century, how our values have changed, what today's successful companies and entrepreneurs are doing and how their decisions reflect the new economy and push it forward.

The economy, new or otherwise, is not so mysterious. It's just the result of what people do for a living. You make choices every day. So do your neighbors, your colleagues, your friends. So do millions of others. Those millions of choices interact. The interaction creates the economy. Today, because people are able to interact across borders and between countries and in virtually every region of the globe, we have a global economy.

Nothing mysterious. If you're going to make a phone call, it's just as easy to call New York as Toronto, or Paris as Montreal. If you're going to take a plane, it's just as easy to take it to Frankfurt as Vancouver—and a whole lot cheaper.

Not only communication is easier. Another fascinating and important change has also occurred: we can now handle a lot more information than we ever could before. Because now, if you're prepared to lay out $3,000 or so, you can have as much computing power on your desk or in your lap as twenty years ago used to fill a room. Why is that important? A couple of reasons spring to mind. First, handling a lot more data comes in handy when it's being generated ten or a hundred times faster than it was when we were kids. But the ability of a computer to compute, sort or analyse is only one of its properties. A computer is also a communications network. We can use it to communicate ideas, and information about anything—engineering, science, art, music, film. And we can communicate those ideas or that information in different ways—numbers, pictures, sounds. We can communicate across the street and around the world. Anyone can do it, from almost anywhere in the world. And this fact brings us the second reason these changes are important. They give us a direct, personal link to the outside world that can't be controlled by anyone else. That's empowerment—personal, individual empowerment. When millions of individual choices result in putting the two capabilities together—computers and communications—on a broad social scale, then we've got a whole new world.

It's this new world and new economy that Canadians today are struggling to master. It's a world that many futurists predicted from the mid-1960s, one that takes us form a society organized around the production and distribution of industrial goods to one organized around the processing and distribution of information. North America is right in the middle of it now—about a third of the 290 million people in Canada and the United States have access to the fifty million telecommunicating computers in individual housholds and companies. But the depth and breath of the changes this new economy brings with it have been masked by four decades of more or less booming economic times.

The new information economy, which is already providing a good living for millions of Canadians, is one that challenges and empowers us to think and act globally. But too many of us are still holding on to a world and a way of living that is fast disappearing.

To gain an even more vibrant, higher quality of life than we remember from the good old days, we need a different mind-set and a modicum of goodwill. All the rest is here. Together with your own imagination, experience and effort, they will provide you with a framework within which to master the changes propelling us forward.

Part One

20 / 20 Visions

One

Canada Near the Millennium

"We're all in this alone"

—Lily Tomlin

BY-GONE CIVILIZATIONS mark their passing with spectacular architecture, like the pyramids, the Great Wall, Notre Dame or St. Pancras Station. But a way of thinking, a way of interpreting events—a paradigm—dies invisibly.

Today's stream of factory closures, job losses, soaring bankruptcy rates, trade disputes and cross-border shoppers look like bad news. Seen through the lens of the old, industrial economy, it appears as though we are slipping backwards, becoming poorer, coming apart at the seams, losing valuable production capacity.

But to those who grasp the new way of looking at what's happening, the unfolding world is full of promise and opportunity. Indeed, never before has each of us had so many sensational opportunities to succeed.

This concept has been stunningly difficult for Canadians, as a whole, to absorb. As a result, we, more than other countries, are struggling with the transition to the new economy. The reason for our reticence is not clear, but it might be that Canada was and is organized like the quintessential industrial empire, around a quintessential industrial technology. All

3

our widely held concepts and all our institutions reflect our essentially late-Victorian beginning—with an overlay of post-war social democracy. Trouble is, the world's moved on, and the life-support system that sustained that kind of place has changed with it.

Too many Canadians still cling to the old ways, because the old ways used to sustain them. Too many others try to capitalize on the anxieties of their neighbors to win more power for themselves—even if what they propose is either impossible or destructive for Canada.

As a community, we have eyes only for the old economy, not the new one. For all their imperfections, we loved the good old days. We knew what made us rich (wheat, trees, energy). We knew what to expect (expansion, growth, steadily improving standards of living). We shared a common vision of our society (our values were tied to material growth and the accumulation of wealth). But appealing as that old world was, it no longers exists. And unless we recognize the present era as a transition, not a dip in the old economy, we will be left with the empty shell.

Let's lay it out up front: this "recession" isn't going to end. It isn't going to end because this isn't a recession.

What this is is the total restructuring of our economy and society. The old economy, which served and sustained us for most of our lives and all of our parents' lives, is at the end of its life cycle. That economy—the industrial economy—is giving way to a new one, which grew out of the old and is growing rapidly. The new economy is not primarily industrial. It's dominated by information—generating it, processing it, storing it and transmitting it. And it's this information aspect that will be the most valuable part of every business.

Howard Cohen, president of the Design Exchange, is an architect who was deeply involved in the development business until it became el supremo oxymoron sometime last year. He says, "The whole Canadian economy has to shift. The ability to create new kinds of opportunities will provide jobs and wealth for the future. If we can't find those opportunities, Canada's going to deteriorate in terms of the quality of life we've all gotten used to." Right on.

This Is What an Economic Transition Looks Like

Gloria Steinem, founder of *Ms* magazine, had a great answer for a reporter who told her he couldn't believe she was fifty. She said, "This is what fifty looks like." Well, this (recession, depression, slowth, tough time, recovery, fill-in-the-blank) is what a transitional economy looks like. It's hard to see through (never mind live through) the difficulties of the current transition, but this is by no means the first structural change ever to have happened. Our economies went through even more difficult structural shifts in the nineteenth century, when local economies were giving way to national ones. Here's a short list. It contains some surprising indications:

- England, 1825–1831. What began with collapsing prices and working-class revolts finished with the construction of the railroads and the opening up of Latin American markets. Those developments ultimately led to the Reform Bill and put the new industrialists in charge of England's public agenda for a century.

- England 1836–1852. This period was racked by a series of crises that saw the expansion of the railroads and the consolidation of the steel business as well as the unilateral adoption of free trade.

- 1857–1869. A series of transatlantic crises began as an accompaniment to the U.S. railway boom, continued through the American Civil War and ended as the telegraph, railroads and Pennsylvania coal and steel created the U.S. continental industrial economy.

- 1875–1900. The last quarter of the nineteenth century was also associated with financial panics as railway building

spread to Europe, and American output began to affect
worldwide prices.

- 1920–1929. The slack early 1920s gave way to the creation of a consumer economy based on consumer
durables, especially the automobile.
- 1929–1980. The Depression ended "people's capital-
ism," creating instead a hunger for big government and
the welfare state that characterized the post World War
II period.
- Post-war economic history is primarily one of expansion
until the 1981–82 recession. Here, too, some interesting
comparisons are in order. For the outcome of that recession was, among other things, the worldwide triumph of
supply-side economic theory.

Let's look more closely at this process of economic transformation. Everything has a life cycle: chickens, trees, people,
products, businesses, industries—and economies. In *20/20
Vision*, Stan Davis and Bill Davidson, who've studied the
evolution of economies, say their life cycles "tend to resem-
ble S-curves, not unlike human life cycles." Economies have
moved from hunter-gatherer, to agricultural, to industrial, and
now to information. "For each cycle, there's an embryonic
phase—a gestation period within the previous economy, like
a child born and reared by adults," say Davis and Davidson.
"From an economic viewpoint, the new-born requires enormous investment and doesn't contribute very much to the
overall economy for several decades."

The one thing that's different about the life cycle of
economies and the life cycle of people is that every time a
new economy is born, the old one doesn't immediately die.
Each economy affects the one before and after it. So today, for
example, even a dry-goods store, the epitome of late nine-
teenth- and early twentieth-century economies, is hooked up
as part of a single system that competes on information: tighter
inventory control, more accurate shelf-space-product turnover

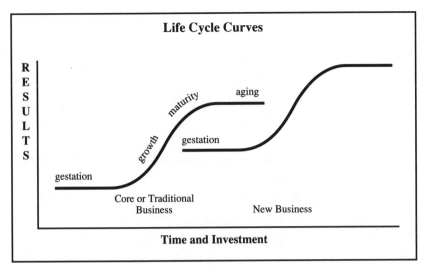

Source: S. Davis and B. Davidson, *20/20 Vision*. Simon and Schuster, New York, 1991.

information, tighter cash management, greater customer throughput, virtually error-free checkout. As Davis and Davidson say, "The end of the fourth quarter of an economy simply means the death of dominance. The sector that lent its name to the economy (agriculture, industry, information) cedes its right to the title. It lives on in the next economy, but only as one of many no-longer-dominant categories."

Ten years ago, when seers like Peter Drucker, Alvin Toffler and others tried to forecast the world of the 1980s, they focused on the broad changes that were then taking place in the economy. Back then, we were told, we lived in a global economy based on information, in which popular tastes had homogenized to the degree that one could truly talk about a global marketplace.

And there was more besides:

• national economic models were irrelevant; only international analysis would be adequate as a basis for decision making;

• natural resources had become uncoupled from economic growth. More output no longer meant more natural

resource consumption. Now we have new materials and knowledge-based substitutes;
*   a new finance economy had emerged with only a distant relationship to the material world of goods production, the result of computerization and other changes.

In the 1980s, all that was coming. In the 1990s, most of it has arrived.

When we know where to look, the shape of the new economy is discernible. Industries that hardly existed a generation ago have become major economic drivers: semi-conductors, computer equipment and telecommunications, for example. Health care industries have developed into another. In these knowledge-based sectors as opposed, say, to more traditional manufacturing like auto parts, Canada's outlook is extremely bullish. Canada is a major player in telecommunications worldwide. Patents granted Canada in information and computer technology in the past several years have exceeded those granted Japan. Canada's health insurance schemes have provided a general health standard higher than that in the United States at less cost, at the same time creating centers of excellence in procedures and equipment.

According to Industry, Science and Technology Canada, the information technology sector has approximately 11,000 firms, which employ 150,000 people and develop and distribute products and services worth more than $17 billion. And as Nuala Beck, a Toronto-based consultant, has documented, more Canadians are now employed in our electronics industry than our pulp and paper industry. More Canadians are now employed in our communications and telecommunications industry than our mining and petroleum industries combined. Almost as many people work in the computer services industry as in the entire air transport industry. Volunteering contributes more to the economy than mines and forestry, utilities and communications— around $12 billion a year, according to a federal government study.

Regionally, too, some major adjustments have already taken place. More Quebecers work in health and medical care than in construction, textile, clothing, furniture and mining industries combined. More Albertans work in financial services than in oil and gas; more people in British Columbia work in telecommunications and communications than in the whole forest industry. More Nova Scotians work as teachers and professors than as fish processors, miners, forestry workers, pulp and paper and construction workers combined.

Other signs of the redirection of Canada's economic efforts show up when we look at different sectors: restructuring of retail businesses to include cross-border holdings in the United States and the elimination of Canadian intermediaries.

Trouble is, Canada is still not internationally competitive in these new sectors the way it is in its natural resource sectors, and the new sectors aren't generating much revenue yet. But it's instructive to compare our restructuring with that of the United States. Because in the United States, the advanced industries are not only major employers—they're also the major revenue generators in the economy.

In the United States, computers and electronics are now bigger businesses in terms of sales than automotive—in fact, since the new cars use a lot of computing power, there are some hidden factors that inflate the automotive proportion. Medical expenditures are bigger than housing (non-farm) expenditures. Hospitals spend proportionately more on information technology than most other sectors: laser surgery, ultrasound, acoustic resonance, sending X-rays over long distance for diagnosis—all these have pushed high technology. People spend twice as much on the phone as they do on airlines (and we wonder why the airlines are having trouble finding passengers). The top four computer companies outsold the top four companies in such sectors as food, beverages, industrial and farm equipment and forest products.

The point is that twenty years ago, these new businesses—

computers, technologically sophisticated medical establishments, a wide range of phone services—barely existed. Now they're among the biggest and fastest growing, and driving the shape of companies as well as determining the kinds of inputs the economy will be using in the future.

Canada is matching these shifts, but too slowly. Michael Cowpland, chief executive of Corel Systems and creator of Corel Draw!, the software program that's likely to become the world standard for computer graphics, sees the decline of the industrial base in the same terms as the decline of the agricultural base: "Seventy percent of Canadians used to work on farms; now it's three percent. Nobody's worried about that because farm work is very heavy and kind of boring. A lot of factory work is similar. Let's do the more interesting jobs which are knowledge-oriented jobs, such as designing software or fashion design or making movies or TV series, writing books..."

The new knowledge-based industries are slowly soaking up our labor force—but they need to grow much faster and bigger if they're going to generate the exports we need to replace the exports we are losing. They need to develop global strategies and a network of profitable overseas affiliates and alliance partners.

Business researchers, such as University of Toronto professors Alan Rugman and Joseph D'Cruz, have discovered that Canadian services have a crucial role to play in improving international competitiveness. In their report *Fast Forward*, prepared for Kodak Canada, the profs show that in the transportation, storage and communications sectors, for example, Canadian levels and growth rates are among the world's leaders.

In a way, it's surprising that these changes have caught the country flatfooted and relatively unready for major change, since two of Canada's major thinkers, both from the University of Toronto, gave us the tools years ago to understand what's

happening to us. Economic historian Harold A. Innis studied
the effects of communication on the organization of empires.
Among his conclusions, presented in a series of lectures
reprinted as "Empire and Communications," was that the shift
from an oral culture (such as that of the ancient Greeks) to a
written culture (such as that of the ancient Egyptians and later
the Romans) permitted the shift from decentralized structures
of empire to more centrally directed ones.

Innis's best-known student, Marshall McLuhan, encapsu-
lated Innis's insights in the phrase "the medium is the message," and gave us the vocabulary for talking about "the global
village" years before it actually arrived. But we're still not
used to describing our country in this way. We're used to
industrial images: assembly lines, blast furnaces, violence on
the picket line. And because our societal heads are in a different
place when we think about what we are, too many Canadians
feel at sea in understanding the enormous changes taking
place in the economy, threatening their life-styles, upsetting
their lives, sapping their ability to seize the moment or enjoy
an improving and sustainable quality of life.

Ready or Not, Here We Come!

In our challenging economic conditions, only the toughest
can survive. To survive, they'll have to lick our imbedded
problems.

Problem #1. Canada suffers from too much institutional
drag—institutions forged by the iron of an industrial age,
evolving slowly over a century, shaped by and reinforcing
the values of an era now past. These institutions, not just the
buildings but the customs and rules that served us so well for
so long, are now limiting our choices as we move into an
information economy and global society. The first big ele-
ment of institutional drag is in the area of government, both

national and provincial. Just how much government do twenty-seven million people actually need? Geoff Poapst, vice president of the Public Policy Forum, a nonprofit group dedicated to excellence in government, says, "It's frightening, just frightening to think of how little experience the people who make economic and fiscal policy have. In the future, the size and role of government is going to be based on its ability to deliver. When institutions don't deliver, they die."

Many individual Canadians seem to be anxious to take up the challenges the transition poses—but they fear that their governments are standing between them and the solutions they seek.

Many Canadians now feel that the center has broken down, and that the federal government is simply no longer capable of developing and implementing the policies Canada needs.

But institutional drag goes beyond government. It encompasses all the rules of the game for the industrial age: the tax system, education, the social safety net, the health care system, transportation, the way we bank, our pension system, the myriad things that have always been there, and that we simply take for granted.

Problem #2. High taxes, high labor costs and a Canadian dollar trading at high levels against the United States dollar are forcing both strong and weaker companies to leave or go under. Jimmy Pattison, one of Canada's most successful entrepreneurs, has put together the fourth largest private company in the country with $3 billion in sales and more than $1 billion in assets. He says, "Our companies are losing customers on both sides of the border because we're not competitive. So we're moving. If we can't make it here now, we want to put our capital where we can get a decent return and where the labor welcomes us with our investment and doesn't fight us... We're also taking layers of management out of our companies...not Band-Aid stuff."

Problem #3. Our education system is so bad that, if allowed

to continue, it will inject more than a million illiterate and innumerate high school graduates into the labor force by the end of the century—this at a time when the workplace is becoming ever more demanding of basic skills.

Problem #4. Our share of world exports is falling. Indeed, while the rest of the world is internationalizing, Canada is not. We should be selling more abroad. And we should be getting more of the things we need from abroad. We shouldn't try to do everything ourselves. According to the Canadian Manufacturer's Association, we've found global suppliers, but not enough global customers. Ten years ago, about seventy-three percent of the goods we bought were domestically produced. Now only about fifty-six percent of what we buy is Canadian-made. That's a sign we're buying much more of what we want outside the country, because we think we're getting better value. But it also means our home-grown producers are losing their domestic market share. They should be replacing it by selling more abroad. Trouble is, a lot of them aren't.

There's only one conclusion: in a world that's internationalizing, the Canadian economy is going the other way. While our major trading partners are getting relatively better at international business, we are getting relatively worse.

Yet this country has a lot going for it and for us. So let's take a look at all the good stuff right up front, because even though this book will take you on a rocky ride over some big potholes, Canada starts out with some huge advantages.

Advantage #1. The United Nations says we live in the best place in the world, bar none. Based on the UN index of national income, life expectancy and educational attainment, we have replaced Japan as the country where quality of life is numero uno. Quality of life is a big plus in attracting top-quality investment. Executives used to European or Japanese cities prefer the safety of Canadian cities to those of the United States.

Advantage #2. The International Monetary Fund says that

next year the Canadian economy will lead the world's developed countries in economic growth. The *Washington Post* wrote a lead editorial not long ago urging the American administration to follow Canada's deficit-cutting example. Investment guru Michael Graham says an "imminent and impressive" rebound in Canadian corporate profits—to perhaps double their aggregate 1991 level—is in the works. This kind of financial heft can pay for the re-equipping and the outward expansion our companies need to export more successfully.

Advantage #3. Despite the trade trends mentioned earlier, it's also a fact that our exports are in a healthy state. We export about thirty percent of what we produce each year, most of it to the United States, with whom we have a chronic merchandise trade surplus. Trade between Canada and the United States has grown steadily, and net foreign direct investment (even after we subtract the outflow of money from plants moving their operations to the United States) is still positive.

Advantage #4. Much as we bitch (skip the next two chapters to avoid the substantive bitches), Canadians, by and large, live extremely well in monetary terms. There may be few of us, but our per capita income—which means nothing more than how much we would each have to spend if we divided the national income by 27 million—is larger than that of people in most countries.

Even in terms of world competitiveness, that 1990s buzzword of advisory committees, politicians and the prosperity initiative, Canada's overall performance is not horrible. To some, that may not be self-evident.

In the most recent annual ranking of twenty-three countries by the Swiss-based World Economic Forum, Canada ranks eleventh, down from fifth the year before. We're weak in industrial efficiency. We demonstrate a perennially sluggish performance in categories such as international and future orientations. These two categories measure the diversity of our export markets and our research and development performance respectively.

This somewhat stinging assessment deserves attention.For these trends to turn around, Canadian management has to get interested in creating knowledge-based products for world markets.

However, there are signs this is occurring. Although Canada's manufacturing sector has a lot of ground to make up, according to Statistics Canada, it scored a surprising productivity jump in 1991 and the first half of 1992. In part, this reflects the Darwinian conditions of recent years. From 1985 to 1990, manufacturing output per person-hour rose 1.7% in Canada, but 16.4% in the United States. But in 1991, changes in business climate forced us to become more productive, and manufacturing productivity surged 6.8% (compared to 1.3% in the United States). By the beginning of 1992, Canadian productivity was rising twice as fast as in the United States. As Nuala Beck points out, "Last year's recession meant a winnowing out. As new orders come in, there'll be fewer suppliers receiving the orders. Instead of ten companies sharing $100 million in orders, six survivors sharing $90 million simply means more orders per survivor."

Other positive consequences flow from thinning the herd. Jobs created in the future will likely be more skilled simply because many low-skilled and low-productivity jobs have disappeared, probably forever. Financially weak companies will be significantly fewer, moving the economic structure toward one of wealth creation from one of wealth consumption. Low-growth, low-return companies will no longer be draining savings, so more money will be available for companies that have the management skills needed for the 1990s. And, assuming entrepreneurs learn from their mistakes, Canada's entrepreneurial pool will be tougher and more experienced.

What the Future Holds

There are still lots of people who aren't participating fully in these changes. They're the ones who feel threatened by what's

going on. Many of them did very well out of the old system—
schoolteachers, public servants, those in protected sectors of
the economy or those in sectors that technology is bypassing, for example huge chunks of the natural resources sector;
middle managers whose main job was to act as information
pipes. These people feel they have to hang on with an iron
grip to avoid being bypassed by the changes taking place
today.

Nothing could be more wrong. On the contrary, the best
way for Canadians to move forward is to embrace change.
And the best way of doing that is to have many more
Canadians understand the nature of economic life cycles, of
the long gestation and development period before the new
economy enters the growth phase when investment begins to
pay off, output accelerates and returns are high.

The decline of the industrial economy does not mean that
the whole industrial sector will die and that there will be no
jobs left at all. All the factories are not shutting down. We'll
continue to have an industrial sector. It will continue to be
productive and turn out lots of stuff. But the factories that
remain will be organized and managed very differently—in
ways that seem alien to traditional industrial managers.

One big difference between the new economy and the old
is that in most countries the link between governments and
national identities is breaking. A new kind of national identity is emerging in Europe and North America, one that relates
to power centers in terms of their functions. In other words,
we're a Canadian for certain things, a Quebecer or Nova
Scotian for other things, a North American for some other
matters, such as trade disputes and Great Lakes cleanups, and
a world citizen for other matters, such as keeping the planet
livable for humans. We have multiplex loyalties that reflect our
generally multiplex relationships.

The responsibilities of governments in areas such as economic
management will also change. Interest rates, currency values and

therefore investment flows and economic growth are mainly determined by the working of the international economy. Governments—especially those in small countries—can't do much about those things anymore. When they try to, they only make things worse. Indeed, the typical national budget has two parts: a confession of past errors, and resolutions to do better next time. The best way to reduce the error is to reduce the function.

Governments will also have to relinquish another area of control: transfer payments from one level of government to another. Instead these will be replaced by private-sector market solutions. In the old industrial economy, governments took some people's money and distributed it to other people. These transfer payments were supposed to maintain local demand so that people could stay in the same place geographically and in the same job category until what used to occupy them was available again. For example, the Hibernia oil recovery project off the coast of Newfoundland is politically motivated to transfer money to the island province so Newfoundlanders can stay there and work. In the private capital market, because of the expense of the oil recovery, Hibernia is a non-starter. Centralized "command and control" government programs and regulations are a legacy of the 1980s. Now, the private market and the information revolution ensure that markets are broad enough and deep enough to operate efficiently. Going to the market to finance a Newfoundland theme park might find some interest, but a mega-project for drilling oil won't. The point is, investment decisions in the marketplace are made on the basis of economic choices; investment decisions by governments are made on the basis of political criteria. Taking politically motivated investments away from government would, in effect, eliminate most of what national government does, except for servicing the debt it and its predecessors accumulated. That's probably what their principal role should be now, anyway.

Government will not disappear entirely. Apart from paying down debt, its central preoccupation will be creating environmental sustainability while helping markets work more
efficiently. It can do the latter by policing out fraud and abuse.
It can do the former by making Environment Canada, not
Finance Canada, the principal department of government.
(More on these points later.)

Possibly even more important than these changes to institutions will be the central shift to a new kind of world in which
the most important wealth-creating instrument is the imagination. This world has always existed to some extent, but only
for some people. Now it's a dominant reality for everyone.
Everyone who has an imagination and has figured out how
to connect it to the marketplace legitimately will prosper.
Others will not do so well.

This is a fabulous, if a little frightening, opportunity.
Remember all those institutions that tried to turn us into good
little industrial workers, or public or private sector bureau-
crats? We don't need to inflict them on ourselves or our children anymore. What we need to do instead is build institutions
that allow people to discover as early as possible the unique-
ly individual magic each of us possesses—and show people
as early as possible how their individual magic can be shared
with everyone else on the planet to make it a better place.
And then that allows them to keep coming back to the well,
both as teachers or learners throughout their lives.

Okay, maybe that does sound a little pie-in-the-sky. But
we're talking about a world in which, even today in some
communities, you can dump a movie down your phone line,
conduct an international discussion with anyone in the world,
watch a soap opera on your computer or videophone—a
world in which imagination is the scarcest good available
in relation to the market to be supplied. Creativity, innovation and ideas are the economic drivers of the information
economy. People who can develop and exploit those

attributes in themselves are scarce, and we may never have an oversupply.

In a planet of five to eight billion minds all hooked up together, there will be, finally, a place for everyone. The problem will not be how to eat. Rather it will be how to conduct the conversation.

In the next chapter, we'll take a closer look at this strange new economy, the new-age, global-information economy that was born when we weren't quite looking. And we'll look at some of the "horizontal" issues—those that cut across everything—that the arrival of the information economy raises.

Two

Riding the Wave /
Catching the Curl

*"The universe is full of magical things waiting
patiently for our wits to grow sharper."*
                                        — *lapel button*

Does the Mantra Have Meaning?

THE WORDS "INFORMATION economy" and "global economy"
have become buzzwords, yet a large number of us don't really know what they mean. Let's look at the information economy first. It grew out of the industrial economy, and the key
idea of the industrial economy is scale: mass production for
mass consumption. The more stuff that comes off the production line (without adding more materials, labor or capital), the lower the cost of each unit of stuff. Think about
Charlie Chaplin on the production line in *Modern Times*. The
cost of each cake he decorated and boxed fell as the production line sped up.

Industrial competition is based on economies of scale.
The companies that survived and thrived were those that
squeezed out a few more items with the same production
workers. They fiddled with the production process to make

it more efficient; they watched each separate procedure to ensure that it fit perfectly into the whole process without a superfluous movement; they measured how much of the various inputs were needed. At the beginning of the industrial revolution, when volumes were small, the observing and counting was easily done by an overseer. When waterwheels ground three sacks of grain an hour, it was no chore to mark that on a slate. Later, as processes sped up, these "control" chores were accomplished manually with electromechanical technology—the stuff invented by Tom Edison and Alex G. Bell: the telegraph, and the telephone—and a large and growing number of so-called white-collar workers, middle managers, clerks and secretaries. These people were generally involved with collecting, analyzing and reporting data.

This electromechanical counting worked fine for about a hundred years. But when processes went faster than the eye could see, the need for better controls, not just to count the output but to deal with the stress on the machinery caused by speeding up the engine, resulted in the use of computers.

Computers started out as clumsy machines that filled a whole room and could be operated only by those with advanced degrees in mathematics. Computers had this fantastic ability to sort, analyze and report, but they were too big and too difficult to use.

Then, some time in the 1970s, thanks to the discovery of microchips and the development of off-the-shelf software that eliminated programming as a requirement, both problems—too big and too complicated—ceased to exist. Instead we had the personal computer, the PC to them as loves 'em. What's more, the suckers could be hooked up over the phone. Result: an economy driven by information processing.

The PC is thus the latest stage in a transformation that began about hundred years ago, as factories began to improve their capacity to control the flow of the materials they needed. The desktop computer brought the control revolution out of the factory and office and down to the individual.

The hooking up of computers and telephones first transformed the world of money. The ability of investment dealers to move hundreds of billions of dollars in a fraction of a second destroyed the power of governments to use the conventional levers of national economic policy.

Once money was liberated, the flow of goods followed. And since people were involved in all this, many of us broke out of our national boundaries, too. Governments have been the last to catch on—they're in a state of continuous post-facto ratification of free trade agreements, because free trade exists anyway; mutual recognition of qualifications, because international companies hire whomever they want in any country anyway; tough monetary policies, because lenders want to lock in high rates of return because their clients demand it, and so on.

The main point is that the control process used to cost industry huge amounts of money. Now the control process has become the central economic activity. It's no longer a cost, it's a money maker. Add to that information-as-new-technology—the knowledge revolution—and you have a new economy.

What Is Information?

Information is more than just "the facts, ma'am." Information is like a liquid that takes the shape of its container. For example, magazines are different from televisions, but they convey the same stuff. Computer networks are not banks, but more and more banking is done over computer networks.

Money is not information. Except that prices, which are a money concept, reflect judgments based on what we know, which is based on access to information. So if and when you go to your friendly neighborhood banker (who may or may not work in a bank), the money you can borrow reflects your expected value in the marketplace, which reflects the information that's known about you.

Let's take a minute to consider how the new communications environment has changed our lives and the way we do business. The best analogy is to the world of transportation. To get around our neighborhood, our cities or the world, we can walk, take our car or a bus, a train, a ship or a plane. No matter what we choose, there's a right of way: sidewalks for people, highways for cars, rail lines for trains, sea and air routes for ships and planes. The world of communications, like the world of transportation, has highways (in this case, electronic highways) with a huge capacity to carry message traffic. And, just as in the world of transportation, the network of communications has evolved unbelievably in the past two generations. When we were children, our choice of communications vehicles was relatively narrow. We had a phone at home. The network over which our voices traveled was the miles of phone lines and the poles to which they were attached. (Although there are still wired phones, they are no longer the only kind, and the wires are going underground.) We could phone long distance, but only with an operator. We had a radio (TV was still a decade into the future), and we had a record player.

Think of all the communication modes that are available in lots of homes today: a mobile phone to walk and talk at the same time (no wires). A message taker. Direct access to long distance. AM/FM radio. TV. Cassette player. Stereo player. CD player. Computer (with or without modem). Video recorder. All these are vehicles for communication, just as certainly as cars and planes are vehicles for transportation. Their networks include microwave signals, optical fibers and satellites. They are all within the price range of the average income earner.

This information-communications environment not only speeds up transactions, it also speeds up the recording and analysis of

those transactions. You buy a shirt or a dress with a credit card.
Is that information? Definitely, yes—the record of that transaction, together with all other transactions, together with similar
information about you and others, creates a data base.

In an information society, you are your transactions. You
can be compared in hundreds of ways, and as a result your
role as a consumer can be described precisely. As well, the
information you supply about your employment is available
in interlinked data bases. Your economic role can be precisely described, as can that of millions of other people.

This information is valuable. Its use is a business. It helps
marketers give you news about new products. It helps companies define new products and services for you and others like
you. It makes data a competitive tool.

Clearly, access to information is power. And, although we
take it for granted, communication has always set the limits
for a society. The following examples, put together by an anonymous source, illustrate this point.

> The Nazi government got hold of radio before the citizens
> did, so there was a top-down bias in the political process.
> But VCRs were legal in Poland several years ago, with
> plenty of rental movies available. We can see what a bot-
> tom-up bias dissident-produced videos did there.

> The Khomeini revolution in Iran was spread by audio-
> cassette and copy machines; no broadcast facility was
> taken over until the Shah left. But in the Phillipines,
> the crucial battle in the overthrow of Ferdinand
> Marcos was for the government-owned TV station.
> The live broadcast of Marcos' inaugural was cut off in
> mid-gesture by the rebels and replaced with a John
> Wayne movie.

> Communication by fax accomplished what nuclear deter-
> rence never could: it toppled communism in eastern Europe

and nearly did so in China. It was a fax news service that kept the outside world informed during the abortive Russian coup. The coup leaders couldn't simply announce to the world they'd succeeded and start mopping up people, as in Stalin's day.

Why Are Computers Central to the Information Process?

Computers let people acquire knowledge, store knowledge, process knowledge and transmit knowledge. It used to be you could do that only with goods—things you can drop on your foot. A piece of ore can be transformed into iron, iron into steel, steel into an auto part. There's value-added in every step. Those who are associated with the value-adding activity can get paid for it. That's industry.

The computer essentially gave services the ability to act like industries. Information—which used to be a service—has now for all practical purposes become an exchangeable good. Knowledge can be transformed and value can be added. And those taking part in the process can be paid. What's more, the people who engage in this activity also acquire knowledge—knowledge of a product and a process. They become valuable. At the end of the day an industrial worker goes home exhausted. The next day he or she is replaceable. Today, just the opposite is true. Companies need knowledgeable employees, and the work depends on knowledgeable employees working in teams. Nuala Beck says, "You're a team player or you aren't... there's no room for hierarchy. There's no pecking order. When you're dealing with knowledge workers, the fact of life is that you manage your knowledge assets differently. In the old economy, labor was the cost of doing business. Labor was a liability... That was the old management structure... that was for the old economy. In the new economy, knowledge workers are an asset. You don't manage your liabilities the same way you manage your assets."

Clearly, accessible information empowers individuals, and through individuals, groups and communities of common interest. It also favors flat, single-purpose organizations over tall, multipurpose ones—for example, Greenpeace or the Environmental Defense Fund or Pollution Probe or any one of the hundreds of single-purpose groups that run bulletin boards and forums on data bases such as Compuserve. These new economy organizations get their information without depending, as they had to in the old economy, on the local press or government or business press releases.

The arrival of the information economy doesn't mean that economies based on the upgrading of natural resources will stop upgrading natural resources. Or that industrial organizations are dead. On the contrary. Manufacturing companies will continue to operate. But they will be run differently. And even though economies of scale are still important, these economies are now managed worldwide, no longer in a single country.

This new economy operates very differently from the old industrial economy. Its technology moves faster than our ability to legislate it. It's physically impossible to impose upon data the same kinds of controls that are imposed on goods and paper-borne information (though we'll likely keep on trying). And unlike a pure industrial company, the new post-industrial manufacturer no longer has such clear boundaries separating itself from its competitors. At many levels, manufacturers are cooperating, for example on the development of new software and in the manufacture of each other's components under cross-licensing arrangements.

Why is this so? Because the speed with which you get your product to market is so critical for success. And because the more people who use a communications product, the more valuable it becomes. These cooperative arrangements, known as strategic alliances, are critical to slash the time it takes to get a product to market and enhance its value by getting a jump on market share. So all alliance partners gain, although in different ways, from such arrangements. The stock market recently valued Microsoft, the world's most important software producer, about the same as General Motors. Yet GM has $123 billion in sales, while Microsoft has $2 billion. Why would the market do that? Quite simply, it is looking ahead: linked computers need software. If motor vehicles are the kings of industrial society, software is the oil of post-industrial society. In Canada in 1992, our telecommunications giant, Bell Canada Enterprises, which uses a great deal of computing power, topped General Motors for the first time ever as Canada's largest industrial enterprise. People would rather telecompute than commute.

Going Global

Another important characteristic of the information economy is that it's global—the result of the myriad linkages built up since World War II to facilitate the circulation of money, ideas and people. Jumbo jets crammed with transoceanic businesspeople is one kind of link. Hooking up phones and computers to churn around $500 billion a day on world money markets has created another kind of link.

Richard Lipsey has educated thousands of young Canadians as the senior author of the book prescribed for just about every university Economics 101 course in the country. Yet Lipsey has now virtually renounced Economics 101 (do we get our money back?) and is out to define a new economic theory that may explain how the economy works. One of the big changes from traditional thinking is the idea that there is only one big economy, not a whole bunch of national or regional ones. Lipsey says: "Examples of globalization are everywhere. Goods markets have become globalized as tastes become more universal, like designer jeans in big cities all over the world. Labor markets are becoming globalized as products are sourced everywhere... Firms are globalizing. No longer do they just have branch plants, but the typical kind of national corporation today is a coordinating unit for whole series of production and trade activities that are spread out, networked across borders. They're much less centrally organized and they spread across borders. Policy is being globalized as the need arises for super-national control of trade, investment, environmental policies, competition policies."

Another person experiencing these changes up close is Jean Monty. Now President and Chief Operating Officer of Northern Telecom, Monty had to move aggressively as chief executive of Bell Canada to deal with a new competitive world from which Bell has been largely sheltered. He says, "We're all starting to look quite differently at our world, as Canadians and, I think, as businesspeople. The Asian evolution of the last ten years, the new Europe and the Free Trade Agreement may not look like such big changes, but a fundamental thing has happened: all of sudden the John A. Macdonald deal of 125 years ago is not going to take us very far any more. The east–west traffic that built this country is not necessarily going to be the basis of our economic well-being in the years to come. So we have to look at north–south traffic and we have to look over the two oceans. And all of a sudden we've become less isolationist, because Canada, whether we liked it or not, was a very isolationist country."

Futurists like Peter Drucker could see years ago that national economic models had become irrelevant for national forecasting purposes; only if you look at the international economy can you have any hope of a sensible basis for making sensible business decisions. Clearly, this has staggering implications for the economic "space" within which governments traditionally operate. The combination of globalization and computerization has completely blown away a great many policy options of national governments. Think of what happens to national interest rate and tax policies in a world in which international investors know more than national forecasters.

Every nation in the world is less sovereign and more interdependent than it was a generation ago. Not only are there no free-standing national economies any more, there are no really national economies any more, either. If you can compete around the corner, you can also compete around the globe. And vice versa. Today, anybody in a small business can operate a global business. Some eighty per cent of Germany's exports are based on small business. North America's largest seller of woodworking tools, Lee Valley Tools, is a small, owner-operated business. Leonard Lee does everything in-house, using new technologies. Susan Murray runs one of the biggest lobbying groups in Canada. She represents business to government, and as a consequence has a broad perspective on business practices. She says, "When you think global, you become global. Sandiline, for example, in Markham, Ontario, exports labels all over the world—the only brand-name sticker in the world. They see themselves as global. They have the most advanced technology in the world; they scout the world for technology. This is a young company and it's not looking over its shoulder. They have product going to sixty countries including Germany, Japan, Taiwan."

Forget the Business Cycle; the Product Cycle's King

The Foundation for the Study of Cycles in Irvine, California, claims there are around four thousand cycles that affect human behavior. These range from astrological cycles to sunspots to business cycles and more. This inventory of cycles shows that all human societies—at least since we shifted from hunter-gatherer to agriculturally based societies—have felt more comfortable with a view of the world that included an alternation of good times followed by bad, followed by the return of good.

The question we have to ask ourselves is whether, in a global, information-driven society, this cyclical view still holds. Certainly many people think it does. The noted United States historian Arthur Schlesinger recently argued for the existence of political cycles in the United States. Virtually every investment newsletter and expert-on-business TV show expects an economic turnaround soon. So surely these cycles must still be with us.

Except they're not. This "recession" is also not a recession. In a recession economic output should decrease. Instead, it is increasing. Indeed, although it's increasing more slowly than we're used to, World Bank economists forecast world output will grow by $7 trillion in the nineties. That's equivalent to thirteen Canadian economies over a decade. So where's the recession? And why is unemployment rising?

One key to what's going on was provided by Peter Drucker ten years ago: namely, that economic growth had come unhitched from growth in employment. In fact, in today's economy, the number of jobless can be increasing at the same time economic output continues to grow.

The fact is, industrial-type business cycles are moribund if not dead. Not because of economics or economic policy. Simply because of technology and the new ways businesses are put together.

In the global information economy, the traditional industrial cycle has been replaced by the product cycle, with massive implications for change in business and all our institutions. Today the leading businesses are based on knowledge—ideas. To be sure, any business is based on an idea. The first big businesses in the United States—the fully integrated meat-packing plants and the frozen rail car transportation grids they needed—all were based on an idea.

But once in place, the idea never changed. It became a formula that was used over and over again. The other costs—capital, labor, real estate—overwhelmed the initial input.

Economic activity was driven by the transformation process—transforming the land, labor and capital according to the original formula—not by the underlying ideas.

The new economy reverses that. The transformation costs are now all functions of ideas: of designs, of production templates, of software. Labor costs, transportation costs, even costs of capital have dwindled to tiny fractions of total product value. A generation ago, eighty percent of what we paid for a new car went to the copper, glass and plastic that was in the car. Costs of materials are still significant, but they don't drive the process. Ideas and their embodiment—in the product itself or in the research, designs and production templates—are what determine product input costs. Today, eighty percent of what we pay for a car goes for the research, design engineering and marketing. Research, designs, formulas, recipes, manufacturing processes like computer-aided design or computer-aided manufacturing (CAD/CAM) are knowledge-based inputs. They are the new economy's raw materials. And they have a startling property—they aren't subject to diminishing returns the way industrial inputs are. To understand why this is so, you'll have to learn a little about the industrial age. (Don't worry, it'll hardly hurt at all.)

In an industrial process, as you add more labor and more capital, your output rises proportionately—to a certain point, after which the output won't increase in proportion to the additions of labor and capital. This is the too-many-cooks-spoil-the-broth syndrome. After this point, more and more inputs produce only diminishing returns. Not so with knowledge-based inputs: the cost of copying a design is zero. No matter how many times you copy the design, the cost remains the same: zero. There is no additional cost to the next copy. (In economists' language, the marginal costs of production are zero.) This challenges all the accepted notions of how to run a company. For instance, how much product should a company produce? In industrial companies, the answer was easy: when the cost of the unit is the same as the average cost of all the ones that have gone before, the optimum production level has been reached. Up to that point, each new unit costs less than the previous one. This phenomenon of declining unit costs is known as returns to scale—the more items you make, the faster you can drop the cost of each item you make. And as long as the cost of each succeeding item is less than the previous one, the more you make, the more your average cost will fall. But at that certain point, the cost of making the next unit will begin to increase. Imagine a factory assembly line stocked with materials and equipment. To produce one item will likely require many workers. So that first item will have a high cost. But successive items will be produced with the same number of workers, so each of those items will cost less. Labor will be hired until the plant is operating at full capacity. At this point, adding more workers won't add to the number of items that can be produced—in fact, returns to scale will fall as the average cost per item goes up.

Information-based products, on the other hand, enjoy another competitive edge—not only returns to scale, but also returns to scope. The more different kinds of product you can create off the same production base, the more you can diversify your markets and reduce business risk. Think of knowledge as capital: a knowledge-based production process that combines economies of scale and scope, in effect uses capital more efficiently. This characteristic has tremendous implications for the traditional industrial business cycle. In fact, it virtually eliminates it.

An industrial firm has only one optimal production point. If a competitor can increase its market by a large share, it can force its rivals' costs upward by forcing it to cut back on production. This situation destabilizes the firm even more. Because employment costs are linked to production runs of single products (economies of scale), a loss of production volume results in the loss of a certain number of jobs. These properties have implications for investors as well. An industrial firm can reach maximum profitability only at a single efficient size. Failure to reach that size affects its ability to reward investors competitively. In other words, a decline in profitability results in a decline in share value and encourages a wave of selling.

The information economy is much more stable. The firm has not only one, but two optimal points. It is profitable at, say, one hundred thousand units of product A, or at one hundred thousand varieties of product A. An information firm can add to its range of products using the same employee base. Having two optimal points instead of one makes employment more stable too.

The competition derives from what's known as the *installed base*—the costs of change to your market. If you're using an IBM PC, you won't be a customer for Macintosh-related products. If you already have a satisfactory spread sheet, you'll be reluctant to change to another. Except that every product has a life cycle.

And that's the key to how cycles behave in an information economy. It's the *product* cycle that counts, not the business cycle. It's the relationship between products that drives the system. No product is perfect. So each product can attack the shortcomings of its rivals. Perceived superior value— including reducing the costs of changeover—drives attack and defense between products, software packages for example, and thus drives the rhythm of cycles in an information economy.

Extending this idea globally, the information economy is something that promises every country fresh opportunities to display its genius to the rest of the people on the only life-supporting planet we know about. The new global economy is designed for people who think big and act boldly—and plan carefully to survive in an unforgiving environment.

Come to think of it, what could be more Canadian than

that? We need to manage the transition away from the old natural-resource economy to one that is much more knowledge intensive. In the next chapter, we explore what lies behind our institutional stickiness.

Three

The Institutional Drag

*The law of holes: if you're in a hole, digging
more efficiently only makes things worse.*
—Bill Davidson

*Leadership is seeing which way the sheep
are going, and rushing to the head of the
flock.*
—Mackenzie King
Canada's longest-serving prime minister

CANADIANS ARE CRANKY. Not all, but many. And angry. And
feeling betrayed. By their governments, by their employers,
perhaps even by themselves. Many business people are baf-
fled, too. A great many are hunkering down and waiting for
things to get back to normal, like the characters in Samuel
Beckett's *Waiting for Godot,* a play about hope that paralyzes
constructive action.

Basically, Canada is held back by a rather large cherished
illusion. (A cherished illusion is one that is held even more
firmly when we know it's contrary to fact because we find it
comforting.) The illusion is that we can deal with challenge
by just saying no. In too many places in our powerful society,
we have evolved a Canadian culture that is a culture of refusal.

35

Our discouraged and tentative embrace of globalization is one example of this. In fact, globalization is a tremendous opportunity for every region of Canada. But lukewarm is as enthusiastic as our policy makers can get. Yves Guérard, chairman and chief executive officer of the Montreal-based management consulting firm Sobeco, Inc., says, "There are many forces of change working on the economy and the Canadian reaction has been to negate them or do nothing, hoping they'd go away." Nancy Riche, Canadian Labor Congress vice president, echoes the sentiment: "There really is a sense of helplessness in the country and people don't seem to know where they're going." Here's how William Dimma, chairman of Royal Lepage, Canada's largest real estate broker, understands the paradigm shift that many people talk about when they talk about the "new economy": "It means that the comfortable pew this country has been living in for perhaps a hundred years or more isn't so comfortable any more. We used to sell our resources at reasonable prices. We imported finished goods. And now, in the past ten or fifteen years, it's a different ball game. Our resources aren't in particular demand these days; other people can supply them. And conservation means those resources won't be used as much anyway. Prices are certainly less than satisfactory. And unless we find some other way as a trading nation, we're out in the cold. There's no point in casting blame... we're all guilty. But governments, businesses, the educational system, the media, all of them together have failed either to anticipate, or to do anything about it."

The world's changing, but Canada doesn't seem to be making the transition. Okay, you might ask, why can't we just ask the government to put a "transition" or "adjustment" program in place. After all, they're in charge, aren't they? Sorry, not really. The new economy has ushered in substantial changes in the ability of any government to pursue domestic policy objectives. Here's how it works: the new economy allows firms to increase in size beyond what one country can support, thus removing them from complete control of any national economy. And, the new economy frees up capital markets so that every government's fiscal and monetary policy can be guessed in advance and allowed for.

Probably the most significant consequence of the combination of globalization and linking of computers and communications is that it snatches away from governments the power to do very much about the pace of economic activity within the boundaries of a single country. Ask yourself, for example, why government economic forecasts and policies are so often wrong. If you're the finance minister in a typical advanced country, you're served by hundreds of economists and analysts whose job each year is to put together a national economic plan. That plan is announced in Canada in the finance minister's budget speech. In the United States, the president's annual State of the Union address serves to signal the nation's economic course.

All the economists are very bright people who've taken lots of courses in economics. Fewer have significant experience of the economy. Generally, the government gets its way and gets its measures through the legislature. (The United States is the exception.) Yet every year the run-up to the budget speech is spent in part promising to avoid the errors of the previous year. For generally, despite all the intellectually high-powered inputs, the predictions—economic growth, public sector borrowing requirement, revenue collected or spent—turn out to be wrong. And of course the unemployment rate is generally not correctly identified and the inflation rate is typically wide of the mark.

Why are all these highly paid men and women apparently unable to come to grips with what's happening? Because the trick can't be done. For one thing, you can't produce sensible economic forecasts for a single country when there are no free-standing national economies any more. As forecasters pointed out in the mid-sixties and later: national economic models are irrelevant. Only international analysis is adequate as a basis for decision making.

Second, and related, international markets know more than national forecasters. In the old, nationally based economies, governments were supposed to control the business cycle by taxing away "excess" demand in good times (collecting a surplus) and running deficits to "stimulate demand" in bad times. The combination of globalization and computerization has completely destroyed these policy instruments. For, if a government gives signs that it will increase taxes, then international business shifts its investments to a place where profits will be better.

You don't have to be a rocket scientist to understand the results: when governments go to the companies for the tax, the level of business expansion has dropped. But the existing business base still needs the extra money to pay the higher taxes, so prices and wages are bid upward and the tax provokes the inflation it was intended to reduce. And if a government suggests it will run a deficit, that means it will increase the amount of money it seeks to borrow. International lenders will withhold money until interest rates become attractive enough to offset the increased inflation risks of the deficit. The higher interest rates demanded by lenders choke off the extra economic activity the deficits were intended to stimulate.

These international lenders aren't just big conglomerates. "They" are us and others like us—lots of individuals who've put our money into offshore mutual funds, or opened bank accounts in the States that we operate through computer programs such as Checkfree, or simply with a Citibank card. Big operators and little, the international economy churns around some $500 billion a day on foreign exchange markets. Decisions taken in the international capital markets are the terminator for state economic power.

This is just one example of how the state's function that we've all taken for granted since World War II is now ripe for change.

You can see the need for change in many areas today. Let's look at three: finance, transportation and telecommunications.

Take Finance (—Please!)

Banking is a federal responsibility in most countries, although some near-bank institutions are regulated at the state or provincial level. The savings and loan (S&L) crisis in the United States showed what happens when a government tries to maintain a nineteenth-century regulatory pattern in the late twentieth century. Billions of dollars flow in from around the world to take advantage of the mismatches and—bam!—the system collapses and the taxpayer pays.

Meanwhile, technology is hopping all the boundaries among banks and making nonsense of the pretensions of regulating capital markets. Canadians can establish bank accounts in the United States and, with their telephones or computers, make all their payments electronically. (Some Canadian banks offer similar services: CIBC is promoting theirs with a nice red telephone and a caption that reads, "This Is A Bank.") And for years we've been able to establish accounts with discount brokers and place orders by computer. So far, not a lot of people are doing this. But everyone could—and probably should.

The banking implications of this are simple: banks will have to compete like everyone else on price, quality and value. They can't rely—as Canadian banks still do—on having the same customer from cradle to grave. More important, it means that the case for national banking systems remains strong on the deposit-taking side, but much less strong on the loan-making side. This situation has very serious ramifications for places like Canada, where regional economic differences are so pronounced. Right now, a banker in Saskatchewan—a depressed region—is able to shift a lot of troubled loans onto the books of the national banking system which is elsewhere more prosperous. Because of our ability to shift loans, our national, or branch, banking system hasn't had the troubles we've seen in the United States. But it also means that the cost of capital in those prosperous regions is adjusted to take account of potential problems in weaker regions.

Well, the smart, computer-equipped banking customer will probably want to deposit her funds where she can get the highest return. But she will shop around for the cheapest credit—which can only come from regions that are prosperous and where cross-subsidization does not occur. In a scenario like this, she would move her savings into national bank branches or a few locally regulated institutions in prosperous regions that are careful about the caliber of loans they make.

There is no question that the markets will sort this out: those local lending banks themselves borrow from the national banks, which have lots of deposits, so interest rates will equalize in the system (or local banks will be acquired by national banks). But the point is that while markets can make these adjustments, jurisdictionally split regulation schemes cannot. These rules will either adjust or disappear—or we'll see more chaos in North American financial services.

The implications of this situation for public policy are enormous. If you or I don't like government policies, we can shift our resources to another location with government policies more to our taste. The only way for governments to take advantage of this situation is to adopt essentially the same standards—which, not surprisingly, is just what they have been trying to do.

The industrial countries have now adopted uniform credit rules for their national banking sectors. And the barriers that remain between different types of financial services (banking and investment dealing in the United States, banking and life insurance in Canada) are crumbling even as we (meta-physically) speak.

Transportation Policy

Similar arguments apply for other areas of regulation as well, such as transportation policy (land, air and water). Since the key to prosperity is access to international markets, cities without direct access are at a disadvantage. This disadvantage will affect the prices of facilities, and thus real estate costs, and thus the tax base in those communities. So increasingly, communities will be planning their economic development programs on the basis of how far they are from the markets, and on the transportation costs of geting there. Pat Lafferty, a principal with Coopers and Lybrand in Ottawa, says, "The transportation system in Canada is not competitive. Go to Rotterdam and see what the Dutch have done with Electronic Data Interchange networking—they're trying to attract business from non-Netherlands countries to go through Rotterdam. You can ship right from Paris to Rotterdam, and the whole thing is paperless right through the customs clearance. Canada still has sixteen bills of lading. Even Canada Ports has different systems in every port. And other modes of transport, like trucks, aren't linked. If they were, we'd probably have a competitive advantage. Seattle's networking electronically. We're not."

Every community will want cheap telephone rates, good road access to major markets and a direct air connection to major international centers. At the moment, the North American regulatory pattern doesn't provide this. In Canada, a great many cities are complaining that they can't get the air service to the United States they need to be competitive across North America. Atlantic Canada is especially badly served. In the United States, the growing concentration of airlines since deregulation means that access between cities is determined on the basis of company hub and spoke strategies. (Cost efficiency in air transportation consists of national carriers serving cities with large potential markets—Montreal, Toronto, Vancouver, Chicago, New York—"hub" cities, and regional carriers—the "spokes"—serving smaller centers around the hub.) The possible (at the time of writing) merger of Air Canada and Canadian Airlines makes sense from the point of view that overheads will be streamlined; but the weakness of the strategy is that Canadian markets are lucrative only because they are still protected from serious competition. Once opened to competition, Canada's domestic routes will cease to generate the revenues they do now. An additional consideration is that the Canadian hubs—Toronto and Vancouver—are stretched to full operating capacity by the present system. They can't handle any more traffic, effectively curtailing growth of the domestic airline market.

The situation on the surface isn't that different from the airborne situation. Canada's passenger rail service provides useful commuting services between some centers, but on outmoded and fragile technology. Bill Stinson, head honcho at Canadian Pacific, spends much of his time arguing that the regulatory environment in Canada guarantees that "freight services aren't competitive with American carriers, and so the quickest route to the border is the strategy of choice for shippers. Canada's most efficient freight network now runs through the United States—both truck and rail."

What's important here is that access costs have the same effect on economic development as a tax. Transportation companies that set high rates in one location and low in another are to a large extent acting as economic development legislators. The current gaps in North American transportation policies are sowing the seeds for conflict in the 1990s, just as they did in the 1880s. In the 1880s, the upshot was that public outrage imposed regulation on the railroads.

If the model of the global information economy described in this book holds, then a clever and workable strategy might be the creation of some kind of North American transportation authority along with a multimodal scheme designed to ensure that every North American community of a million or more inhabitants has direct access to major international hubs. God knows what the years-long deliberations of the Royal Commission on Transportation will be. But playing a key and determining role in the evolution of a North American multimodal transportation policy is the vision of choice. That's the logic and the power of the new economy.

Telecommunications

To drive home the point a little further, let's take a refresher on this one. In Canada, our regulatory pattern is based on keeping different telecommunications technology separate: voice and data, video, cable, broadcast and so on.

Telecommunications policy is evaluated from the standpoint of preserving culture instead of from the standpoint of what the technology can do to help people. This policy is so fundamentally unworkable that Canada's regulatory framework is already in tatters. And it's going to get worse. Here's why. In the 1990s, we're witnessing a convergence among all telecommunications providers, including phone companies, computer companies, cable TV companies and information providers. The world of information is on the brink of transformation. TV networks, news organizations, universities, writers, researchers and users—all those distinctions are now obsolete: there is only information, and you can have it any way you want it. News on the telephone, chats on the computer. In fact you can do that now.

In the information economy, the information component is stripped off products and transmitted worldwide in seconds. For example, investment dealers use computers to reformulate credit instruments for international capital markets. Governments and corporations that want to borrow money issue bonds. The bonds are the raw material. Then the traders go to work: they strip off the interest rate coupons and sell them separately to investors prepared to pay for an income investment. They sell the coupon-stripped bond to other customers who want to invest for capital gains. There are as many variations on these themes as there are customers, because computers can transform raw credit into investment portfolios customized to match the high-reward or minimum-risk strategies of the investors. Bringing the technologies together turbocharges the process. The convergence among different information technologies is a simple fact of engineering life. The issues that convergence raises are far from simple. There are hundreds of them and there's only one way to resolve them: the market. The collectivity that is the market is a categorical imperative because the choices are too complex for the state to regulate. The state's attempts can do harm by distorting the choices involved.

If this sounds a little mysterious, ask yourself this. Why don't we watch our phones and converse over the television? Only because the regulators don't let us. But in fact the telephone, the private branch switch in the office wall, the computer with a modem on your desk and your television set are basically the same instrument. Thanks to digitization, all information terminals—phones, computers, TV sets, radios, telexes, faxes, you name it—essentially tap the same water from the same pipe. They provide information to people who need it: people get the information and use it to buy a plane ticket or a piece of a company. The phone or computer or fax all add organization to information. Logically, they're in the same value chain—and therefore in the same business. The issue for regulators, then, is to explain why the processes should not be combined in the same companies. Right now, that's illegal. The regulations force an artificial separation between television and telephone.

This is unreasonable and impossible to defend. What if the phone company were to go ahead and give everyone in Winnipeg, Montreal, Halifax, wherever, a video dial tone and let them run their TV sets, phones and computers over the same lines? Would the CRTC issue a warrant for the arrest of the head of the phone companies? Anyway, while the cops were worrying about that, someone else could just put a satellite up over St. Paul, Plattsburg, Boston, you name it, and offer half the service—the sending half— at less charge. And smart Canadian office buildings with a satellite link or even a microwave transmitter could bypass the telephone network altogether. In fact, that's happening now.

The point is that this aspect of the information revolution— the convergence of telecommunications technology—is another death blow for the way Canadians currently do things. One way or another, things have to change. A new framework is essential. But to get that framework, there has to be at least a majority in favor of some particular solution. Hence the current strains.

What Is the Role of Government?

Confronted with the scale and scope of change implied by these economic and technological forces, the question arises, why doesn't government try to get ahead of the curve? Many of those interviewed for this book expressed considerable frustration on this point. Hugh McDiarmid, chief executive of Stormont Investments, says, "The role of government is to tear down the institutional barriers that have created the very nice, protected enclave." His partner and chairman of the board, Rod Bryden, says, "We have too many areas in which government has assumed that because something would be good to do, it should therefore do it... Canadians don't need that, can't afford it, and don't want it."

Lloyd Barber, former commissioner of native land claims, says that "until governments really get involved in the electronic age and the universality of communication, in the value of knowledge qua knowledge, they're increasingly obsolete." Political lobbyist Susan Murray agrees: "Our frustration with Canadian governments—all of them—is that they're not moving fast enough to get rid of regulatory barriers. They're absolutely obsolete, in a global economy." Geoff Poapst, vice president of the Public Policy Forum, an organization devoted to excellence in government, talks about the public service as "a threatened industry... The proud, confident public service that was, say, the best in the world in the 1960s was suited to the 1960s environment. And it's not suited to the 1990s environment."

Even experts on the public service and former public servants themselves talk about how difficult it is to make something happen. David Seibel, consultant with Arthur Andersen, says, "I think some people within the public service are probably capable of dealing with the new paradigm. But the leadership to take them from where they are to where they have to go is evolving too slowly. If managers and leaders don't recognize that they have to help the people deal with the change, then it'll be a failure."

One problem is that too many managers and leaders think the search for new ways of doing things should not apply to defining the public purpose and expressing it. In fact, there's every reason to think that public policy management is undergoing the same wrenching changes as private enterprise.

"After the Revolution..."

We're already seeing the development, particularly in North America, of a kind of cafeteria of public bodies. You go to whichever one you think will do you the most good. Say you're a Quebec-based businessperson wishing to export to the United States. Ideally, you want to go to one place to resolve all your problems, but as things stand now, there is no one place: there are many. The Quebec Ministry of International Affairs has programs to help you. So does the federal government. So do the American states. Too many "helpers!" This situation is too complex and needs to be streamlined.

The same problem exists with the approval process for new products, especially in health care. It also applies to professional qualifications, environmental standards and a host of other issues. There's enormous pressure for simplification from the people who have to thread their way through these pathways today.

One way to accomplish the simplification is to make the rules that apply in one jurisdiction acceptable in all other jurisdictions, even though each jurisdiction may continue to have its own rules. This formula is now in use in Europe. Interestingly, it came about through the court system, not through legislative action. Even in Europe, where the commitment to a single economy receives daily rhetorical homage, the political system was unable to cut through the web of interests to deliver commonly agreed standards. One way or another—whether by courts, by contracts among companies or by some other means—economic pressures will push North America toward mutual recognition.

Many people worry that mutual recognition means that the lowest denominator—that is, the lowest standard—will become common. But that's not necessarily the case, for two reasons. First, the quality revolution sweeping corporations is pushing them toward a zero-defect standard for most products. They will not accept lower standards. Second, the public will learn to consider place of origin as well as costs when it buys a product or service. If Mexico is associated with toxic chemicals in food, consumers will avoid Mexican food products even if they cost less. How will they know? Well, in an information society, there's lots of information available, and

lots of people able to supply it to those who don't want to get
it themselves.

The Impact of Federalism

For many states—and especially for federal states—the new
economy is causing a crisis of legitimacy, too. This is especially true in Canada, because the need to service one of the
highest public debt loads of the western economies constitutes the major strain on our capacity to adjust our economic base to these new forces. We incurred most of the debt
before this new economy really began to bite. Now, when
governments have many fewer policy levers than before, we
have to pay it down.

The impact of these pressures on federalism has been to
divide the country along its historic fault lines. Quebec is
more socially cohesive, and more economically vulnerable
than some other regions. It feels it really must get on with the
job of adjusting to this new economy. It fears the retarding
effects of an Ottawa whose constitutional powers now exceed
its capacity to deliver. So it wants massive decentralization
of those powers... or else the chance to go it alone.

Ontario and points west perceive their vulnerabilities in historic terms as well—their principal fear is absorption by the
United States. So they want a "strong central government" to
help them resist the attractive power of the United States. Then
there are the unacknowledged layers of government that no
one understands but which nevertheless play a vital role in
shaping Canadian policy: the myriad consultative groups that
interact among the different traditional layers of government.
A similar structure is also emerging on a North American basis,
comprising relations between provinces and American states,
as well as overarching bodies for resolving common problems.

For countries as regionally diversified as Canada, the job of
managing the economy is particularly difficult, now that the

conventional relationship between sectors has also broken down. Once upon a time, Canada's regions together acted as a portfolio of investments such that each contributed to a greater pie: cheap food from the prairies meant a healthier manufacturing sector; depressed manufacturers meant cheaper prices in the resources-based regions; a surge in demand for the products of one region created demand for the products of the other regions. The whole thing balanced off at year's end with centrally directed transfer payments.

No longer—in fact Canada's economy hasn't worked like that for about ten years. Today, Canada's regions hurt each other—by adding to government spending—but don't help each other much because they buy resources and parts from other countries, and because technological change means resources are no longer automatically linked to manufacturing output.

Collective Identities Are Complex

The information revolution is also posing a number of looming changes in the area of collective identities. Asked what community they belong to, most people find it hard to give clear answers. We're Canadians, sure, but we're also citizens of Ontario, Quebec, British Columbia, and so on. So sometimes we disagree and do things differently from "Canada."

Besides the Canadian thing, we're also North Americans and we look to North American systems (which are rapidly developing) to regulate such things as cross-border pollution, common rivers and lakes, and trade disputes. And we're doing this despite what our individual national legislatures say. Indeed, on trade matters, we've seen both Canadian and particularly the United States governments become increasingly irresponsible because they know that our binational and multinational arrangements will take the political heat for straightening out goofy protectionist measures afterward. The new economy is already growing supranational authorities, so local politicians can play to the folks at home, while the transnational bodies make the rulings that stick.

And, beyond North America, we're also citizens of this beautiful planet. When it comes to taking care of it, we want some planetary systems to be effective.

These different loyalties are not that new and, like federalism, we used to arrange them in a kind of hierarchy or layer cake: one layer of authority for local matters, another layer for provincial, yet another for national and still others for international. But an information economy doesn't layer.

You've basically got torrents of electrons pouring around the world waiting for individual consumers to pull down as many or as few as they want to use. For instance, the TV shows you watch are regulated nationally, whether U.S. or Canadian. But if they contain financial information about stocks, the norms for that are set nationally in the United States and provincially in Canada. Americans watching *Business World* on CBC's Newsworld may be able to complain to Ontario, if the matter is about equities, or nationally, to the Canadian Radio and Telecommunications Commission, if it's a broadcast matter.

Canadians with a complaint against Louis Rukeyser's *Wall Street Week* would appeal to a U.S. national regulatory agency—the Securities Exchange Commission (if the issue is equities) or the Department of Commerce (if the problem concerns commodity futures) or the Federal Communications Commission (if the issue affects the broadcast license.)

Take phone calls. While it's true that international phone rates are the result of agreements between countries, companies who buy phone-line capacity at bulk rates for sale to customers, along with innovative services—called resellers—are now able to use computerized switching to route international calls around locations where long distance rates are lowest. So even though the phone company and the domestic rate-setting tribunal may want you to pay x cents a minute to call between two centers, a smart phone reseller may be able to connect you for less—it's just that the call may go via New York or Hong Kong!

The upshot: there are no consistent layers in the cake anymore. Instead, government authority in an information economy is all mixed up, like a marble cake, a strudel, a stew.

The chapters that follow are like a marble cake, too. The various industries and institutional arrangements that have evolved over the past hundred-odd years have served the needs of the industrial era phenomenally well. Indeed, so well and for so long that we've come to believe that this is the way it always was, or that "this"—universal medicare, social assistance, unemployment insurance, even a job—is an entitlement. What follows is a new economy perspective on transformation options for twenty-first century success.

Part Two

Rethinking a Global Information Economy

Discovery consists of looking at the same thing as everyone else and thinking something different.

—Albert Szent-Gyorgyi

IN THE NINETEENTH century, the typical occupation of a prime age male (the only human who counted in the money economy) was that of farmer. Today, fewer than three percent of the population call themselves farmers. For most of the twentieth century, the typical occupation was that of blue collar, industrial worker. Fewer than twenty-five percent call themselves that today. Neither the agricultural nor the industrial sector has disappeared. Prominent perhaps, but no longer dominant.

Societies work because they have rules that everyone understands, codes of values, ways to behave. Maybe we don't subscribe to all the written and unwritten rules we live by, but we thought we knew what they were, what was expected of us. Canada's institutions—the ways we deal with particular issues, from redistribution of income to education to governance—evolved from and reinforced our values—the values of the industrial age.

Now the game is changing rapidly, and the rules we played by aren't appropriate for the new game. But the task of trying to fit the new realities into the old framework is proving more difficult than anyone imagined. The old rules and old ways of looking at things are getting in the way, caging us in, holding us back from a smooth transition to the new economy.

This section offers a new perspective on a number of old industries and institutions. It's not a forecast of what's likely to happen, but a look at how what's already happened is creating the future. It's meant to give you a "whack on the side of the head," to use Roger von Oech's phrase. Von Oech is head of a California-based (where else?) firm that helps people become more creative. "When things change," he says, "it's no longer possible to solve today's problems with yesterday's solutions." So you have two choices: bitch like hell that things aren't as easy as they used to be, or use your creativity to find new answers and ideas that will help you match your strengths to the changes, thereby defining your own potentials and opportunities.

Many of us need to unlearn what we know, because as long as we think we know the right answer, or as long as we believe "this is the way things are done," we'll never look for another answer or another way. Treat this section as a selection of possible right answers. As you read it, you'll undoubtedly think of other answers. Inventor Ray Dolby (as in the Dolby system, which took the hiss out of recorded music) says inventors "don't jump at the first solution because the really elegant solution might be right around the corner. They just keep on thinking."

Four

The Industrial Economy
in the Information Age

"Variables don't, constants aren't"
                    —*sci-fi lapel button*

As EXPLAINED IN Chapter 2, one of the major differences
between a global, information-based economy and the national industrially based economies of old is the fact that the business cycle has given way to the product cycle. Shorn of fancy
jargon, economic activity is slow because only some of the
products available are exciting buyer interest. What determines the pace of economic growth in today's economy is
nothing more or less than the ability of new and established
products to find buyers. Forget the rest.

Not that overall output doesn't continue to rise and fall. In
the past, that rhythm was the result of a mismatch between
investment and savings. Depressions arose when money that
should have been invested in new productive facilities was
instead saved outside the system. It was saved in backyards or
under the mattress—because people had lost confidence in
their banking systems. Once that problem disappeared—which
it pretty well did after World War II with the institution of
deposit insurance—there were, in fact, very few technical

recessions. Indeed, even two major stock-market meltdowns, in October 1987 and October 1989, failed to make much difference to economic activity.

To understand what's happening in today's stagnant business climate, you have to realize, among other things, that the Cold War is over, and military spending, which was already tracking downward in real terms, is now declining even more quickly, especially in Europe and the United States. In the United States, defense spending is down about nine percent in 1992 over 1991, not accounting for the Gulf War.

As a result, there have been lots of layoffs, especially in the high-tech sectors, along Boston's Route 128, in Seattle, Florida, Texas and California. These are among the motors of the U.S. economy. Fewer defense products means a major decline in economic activity. And let's not overlook the absence of inflation. After four decades, it's not just product prices that are flattening out, it's assets, as well. Land and property prices have been trending down for several years; Japanese share prices have fallen for close to two years; European and North American stocks have been flat for almost as long.

Asset deflation has a domino effect. When the value of your house and retirement income goes down, you don't feel like spending much. Financial institutions are rethinking their lending criteria as they struggle out of the loan-loss provisions they had set up to cover the bad loans they made to the industrial economy during the 1980s. They base their lending on the value of the collateral you offer as security, so they lend less.

Demographics aren't helping. Most people are (or soon will be) through the family formation stage—the stage when people buy lots of consumer goods. That was happening a lot ten years ago. Now, with fewer children in school or university, family-related outlays are pretty restrained. Take a look around your own home. You probably have all the TVs you want, likely a VCR and a microwave, a car or two in the garage. You probably bought or replaced these things within the past five years—that is during the 1980s. You don't need any more. There's a slightly lower probability you have a home computer or a video recorder. And if you got one, it likely was a replacement for an older one. So there is very little pent-up consumer demand to replace the demand for military output.

Look at the services side, which now represents about seventy-five percent of Gross Domestic Product in most advanced economies. In considering this side of things, we should bear in mind that a great deal of reorganization has been going on in the corporate sector: many middle management jobs have been lost as companies pare down to their "core competencies" and seek "strategic alliances" for more cost-efficient ways of doing many of things they used to do in-house. What happens to middle managers laid off in midcareer with a good bonus? Many have become consultants or bought franchises. But others find it hard to do this as banks cut back on their lending. If we consider the North American market as a single entity, the American savings and loan crisis—mainly the result of poor public policy—is taking somewhere between $U.S. 200 billion and $U.S. 500 billion in capital out of the system—that is, a factor ranging between thirty-five and ninety percent of the Canadian economy. This development is matched by a drop in real estate values, so that your equity in your house has probably shriveled by quite a bit, depending on where you live. This cuts down on the amount of borrowing and lending that can be done.

Finally, look what's happened to advertising: half the mass audience has deserted the advertising-financed television networks like CBC, CTV and Global for cable, like CNN, and is heavily into using its VCRs for time shifting. As for commercials—zap, fast forward, please. As a result the mass advertising essential to promote mass consumption is dying on the vine. Most promotional dollars are spent in stores differentiating products, not on getting people to go to stores. So people don't go: instead they go to discounters who promote heavily to lure people off their couches.

There's very little about this situation that is cyclical. Rather, you can see that without something really exciting to buy, rational consumers would rather maintain a little liquidity—keep their cash, thank you very much.

If you look at what is doing well now, you can also see the hand of the product cycle at work rather than the business cycle. People are buying computer software, using the telephone, seeking nonbank financial advice, and they are concerned about the quality of food and health care. These areas are all moving ahead on a North American basis. These sectors reflect the aptness of the products for the times: the fabulous success of Microsoft Windows, to make DOS computers easier to use; the fabulous success of Corel Draw!, which is becoming the graphics standard worldwide; a drop in business meetings and a preference for faxing; a growth in services that give financial advice upon separation from company, spouse or both; and a general obsession with cholesterol and aging. Producers of successful products in those areas generally aren't aware there's a slump.

Where Do People Fit In?

Remember the bumper stickers and lapel buttons of the 1960s? One read, "I am NOT an IBM card: do not fold, staple, spindle or mutilate"—an obviously widespread concern about loss of identity in the wonderful world of post-war automation. In the library of books and articles on the global information economy, very little has been written about its effects on the lives and careers of ordinary working people.

Economists speak of transitions and adjustments, the way generals speak of kill ratios. For the well-educated and those with professional skills, the future may mean a little less, or perhaps a little more. But for those in traditional, resource-based sectors or heavy industrial sectors, those with lots of work experience and little else, we're talking finito. It's over. Where these jobs still exist, they will have become third-world jobs and will generate third-world wages. You can't live on third-world wages in Canada.

Conventional wisdom nevertheless says that the combination of globalization and computerization is shifting jobs to the service sector and dividing those jobs into two categories: high-paid professional jobs, such as investment dealing, and low-paid, minimum wage jobs, which can become one-way tickets to a life spent in working poverty. The Economic Council of Canada, now defunct, warned of this shift in a recent study called *Good Jobs, Bad Jobs*, and it used its findings to persuade young people to stay in school as long as possible. For in today's knowledge-based economy, learning is capital. Those with a lot of it have a good capital endowment.

But the good-jobs bad-jobs conclusion is the end of the story only if you look at the world through glasses tinted with an industrial society perspective. If you change that perspective to one more appropriate to an information society, you can see that something very different is really going on.

"Modern" economics—the stuff that's being taught across the country to unsuspecting youngsters—began with Adam Smith around the time of the American Revolution. Smith, circa 1776, traced the causes of the wealth of nations to, among other things, the skill and ability of the work force. This perspective reigned supreme until economic theory began to change around the last quarter of the nineteenth century—at about the same time there began to be really sizable companies, mainly huge transcontinental railroads, and enormous iron, coal and steel combines. It was around that time that economics began to transform workers from their previous position as the central factor in the creation of wealth to being just another factor in wealth creation—along with land and capital. The "land, labor and capital" that everyone in high school learns are the "factors of production" became so only about a hundred years ago.

Since then, in the period we can now refer to as the "industrial age," the creation of wealth has been seen as the result of efficient markets in which labor, along with other production factors, received a return equivalent to the value it added at the margin (that is, the value it added to the next unit produced). At the same time, the design of the factory and of production processes was aimed at "deskilling" the work force, at breaking down the barriers between industrial crafts and unskilled work. The idea was to make workers as much like identical parts of a machine as possible.

Stephen Blank, Director of Canadian Affairs, Americas Society, New York, says that at the very beginning of the Industrial Revolution, before the introduction of common measurements and the assembly line, "the guy who assembled the car was a highly skilled worker. He had an intimate relationship with the product, and the process; but he couldn't buy the thing he was making because it was one of a kind. It was too expensive." Then came standard measurement and production lines, and economies of scale—and deskilled workers. Prices of industrial goods started dropping. In the newly organized world of a hundred years ago, says Blank, "The guys on the line plugged in, they turned this, they did that, they pulled something. But at the end of the day, they could buy the products they were making. And that was an enormous change in our whole society. It created a whole new kind of worker: the industrial proletariat. It created cities, it created classes and ultimately because the state aggrandized this production function, as well as a rising state in a period of great conflict, it created the modern nation states."

Now, in the knowledge-based economy, we find that the old industrial economy way of figuring out how the economy works no longer properly accounts for wealth creation. Stephen Blank sees parallels between what's happening today and what happened in the 1870s and 1880s. The invention of production lines changed not only the way people made goods, but the way society itself was organized. In particular, people were downgraded from skilled to just another cost of production along with new materials and money. Now, in a knowledge-based economy, people have again become assets. The more they know, the more valuable they are. When a really valuable employee leaves, the value of the company that loses him measurably declines. This has happened in numerous takeovers during the last decade. When the new company proved an unwelcome master for the knowledge worker of the acquired company, he or she walked. Result: the acquirers were left with a lot of bricks and mortar. But the company they just acquired had walked out the door.

The most exciting thing about this development is that we can't marginalize the knowledge worker. True, his or her knowledge can become obsolete. But if he or she keeps up with the field or a number of fields, he or she will always be an asset. Knowledge workers go home tired. But they also go home a little less replaceable than they were the day before—provided they aren't just passing knowledge along, but are actually adding value. The middle managers who have been shed in great numbers over the past few years were mostly just passing knowledge along.

People who transform knowledge to make it more valuable often don't need the company that hires them. If the company disappears and they're on their own—well, they'll survive. They're like professionals in any setting: lawyers, accountants, but also computer trainers, desktop publishers, programmers, data-base searchers, and so on. The key point is that they have to add value—and for that, some training is needed. Nancy Riche is a tough, uncompromising and intellectually honest vice president of the Canadian Labor Congress, which, at least for the moment, represents more than two million unionized workers in the country. She says, "We don't think that the employer, the business community if you like, has reinvested enough in either research and development or worker training." She's not alone. The Economic Council of Canada chastised business more than once for not putting sufficient money into on-the-job training.

What does it take to become a knowledge worker? Do you have to have a PhD in something? Or is it a career open to everyone? Well, the nice thing about computers is that they're getting more friendly, and a lot smarter: the programs are usable by almost anyone. Michael Cowpland, visionary founder of Corel Systems, says, "We do have our share of the rocket scientist type—we're always looking for those—but they're leveraged very well by the rest of the organization. We don't need as many of the computer science degrees and the heavy-duty PhDs. See Arlan over there? I think he had a degree in history or geography. We get people with general backgrounds, bright people from different areas who like computers and aren't afraid to use them. We just need dynamic people, and they can have quite a wide variety of training."

What companies don't need are people who spend a lot of time passing information along a complicated chain of command. The company has to be able to turn on a dime. To be a fighter plane, not a bomber. So there can't be a lot of people around just relaying messages. Everyone in the firm must add value to the chain, or else they're out.

If an organization has one layer, the boss can find out what's going on in one conversation. But after that the number of conversations increases faster than the layers of management. To illustrate: if the organization has two layers, there must be three conversations: CEO to Manager Norm. Manager Norm to Manager Douglas. Manager Norm to CEO. With three layers, the chain is: CEO to Nick, Nick to Marnie, Marnie to Cam, Marnie to Nick, Nick to CEO—five conversations. With four layers, there must be seven conversations.

Each time you add one layer of management, you add two conversations—and each time you cut one layer, you accelerate the information flow by two. This arithmetic is the terminator as far as middle management is concerned. Even without advanced technology, global firms have to flatten out. The competition demands it. But we do have advanced technology, and here's where it comes in. Computers make it easier for CEOs to find out directly what's going on. They don't need five or seven layers of management to ask. They can go directly to the data, if they have a computer in their office and they know how to use it.

Quick Nickels Is the Name of the Game

Companies and brand managers know that getting product to market at the right mix of price and value is the name of the game. That is how companies compete. Product cycles have consequently shrunk from something like five years in the leisurely 1970s to two years or less. For most companies now it's a game of quick nickels. No time to wait for slow dollars. Canadians are struggling to accept the idea that today the product cycle has succeeded the business cycle as the main determinant of economic results. If you make something the world wants, you'll prosper. If you don't, you won't. And if you rely on selling intermediate products to others who make the products that drive the economy, you're in a diminishing returns game. Because every corporate strategist is following Harvard University guru Michael Porter's advice to minimize dependence on a single supplier. Because every firm must cut costs to survive, and many intermediate products can probably be bought more cheaply outside Canada. It's hard to say why such a simple idea is so difficult to understand, but it may have something to do with our economic culture and its increasing irrelevance.

From sea to sea to sea, Canada has, for most of its history, been about natural resources—staple commodities destined for imperial markets. As a nation, we've never been great transformers of raw input into finished products. Rather we're great transformers of harsh landscape into mines, commercial timber operations, oil and gas wells and pipelines—sagas stored in the soul of every Canadian. And, as Michael Porter's recent review of the Canadian economy shows, our export dependence on resources is actually growing while exports in other sectors decline.

About forty-six per cent of our output today is natural resources, mainly in an unprocessed or semiprocessed commodity-like state. Our competitiveness in this field is waning, as it is in manufacturing. Manufacturing, mainly auto-related, constitutes our major source of manufactured exports. These are under tremendous cost-competitive pressure. Canada attracted more than its share of automotive production capacity in the 1970s and 1980s. In the 1990s we'll probably have to shed a portion of those gains. The public policies and mind-sets governing the conduct of these sectors—that is, the kinds of activities we encourage or discourage with taxes, subsidies, accounting protocol and customs—are not likely to lead to easy transitions. For one thing, our investment patterns will have to change to take into account the changing global environment. We overinvest in natural resources. We underinvest in people and ideas, especially in skills upgrading and technology. Our investment growth is high, but it's not the kind that's linked to high productivity. Worker training, research and development as a percentage of gross domestic product, machinery and equipment investment—all trail those of our major international competitors. Says Lloyd Barber, dean emeritus, University of Regina, "We've been bloody good hewers of wood and drawers of water. For 125 years or more, we've been very, very successful at living off our capital. We better wake up fast: world economic slowdown, and this fundamental paradigm shift to something else, means that living off our capital is no longer giving us a fat and happy life."

Meeting the Challenge of the Future

We used to sell our resources at reasonable prices. We imported finished goods. Now it's a different ball game. Our resources aren't in particular demand; there are other people who can supply them; there are new materials to substitute. And conservation in a number of areas means that the resources won't be used as much, anyway. Prices are certainly less than satisfactory.

Clearly, the natural resources sector will continue to shrink as a wealth producer. To continue to exploit it means transforming the way it is organized. Brainpower will determine whether we meet the competitive challenge of inventing new uses for old raw materials. Says Yves Guérard, chief executive of Sobeco, a Montreal-based management consulting firm, "We need to exploit our natural resources in a more advanced and more technological way." There are models for us to emulate. The Finns, for instance, also have forestry, but instead of simply shipping logs, they've developed not only a better way to manage their forests and get more wood out of a smaller area, they've also built a whole industry around that. They're world suppliers of equipment for handling timber and cutting it. They've built on the expertise they have in forestry because they started with a forest, and they've used it to become suppliers of forestry high-tech.

Moving Out of Natural Resource Exploitation

Economic futurist Nuala Beck says closing down our natural resource sector would be stupid. Argues Beck, "The new economy is as metal-intensive as the old economy that it's replacing. Mining was a major supplier of the commodities we used in the old economy, and they're major suppliers of some of the major metals that are used in the new economy."

Beck's analysis highlights two components to our competitive challenge. First, Canada's always been a major commodity exploiter. We had phenomenal growth because we were a major supplier of the major commodities that were used in countries that were good at manufacturing. We got dragged along in the wake of forty spectacular years of growth. Now, says Beck, we're emerging, once again, as a major supplier of the commodities that are being used in the new economy. "And we're going to get dragged along in the wake of spectacular growth in the next twenty, probably thirty-odd years."

The second component of our competitive challenge is that we also have an emerging new economy. Beck's research confirms that "Canada has three of the four engines of growth in the new economy: communications and telecommunications, electronics, and medical and health technology. Instrumentation is the fourth. That's not bad at all. We have world-recognized competitive advantage in things like communications and telecommunications. Canadians are probably the last to realize that, but the fact is we have global strategic advantage there. And we have a huge electronics industry in this country that's the best kept secret as far as I'm concerned."

How and To What Should the Transition Be Made?

It doesn't take long to figure out where to start. For all the bitching we do, we start with a base of trained and educated and technologically astute people, a capital base and an infrastructure, including things such as hospitals, schools, roads and airports and stuff, that are competitive on a world basis.

We can produce a very interesting cultural, intellectual and spiritual home for people as long as we permit our regional economies to compete globally. We can't compete as a single economy—we're too diverse. Public policy has been inappropriate because we've felt that we should be able to do what the Germans do and the Japanese and the Americans do. We can't. What we can do, in relatively small, regional circumstances, we do extremely well. But let's not think that because the west can produce beef and wheat, and Quebec has competitive electric power, and there are pockets of high-tech the rest of the world wants, that therefore Canada can produce everything competitively with the rest of the world. It doesn't work that way.

Jean Monty, President and COO of Northern Telecom, former chief executive at Bell Canada, knows it doesn't work like that. "I'm starting to look at how we, from a Canadian base, can become a participant in this global economy that is taking shape. And particularly North America. At this stage let's be realistic: we are very close, we have a four-thousand-mile border with a huge country, and we have to have a small country strategy." That means being good at trading resources, because resources are what we've got. It means being good at the services we're good at: pipelines, financial services, telecommunications. There's an interesting case developing in the aviation industry, with Bombardier and CAE Electronics and with CITA in Montreal. Governments have already spent enough to make Bombardier a solid and very successful company. We don't need to send them more money; we do need to put the environment in place to let them grow.

Once upon a time we had a powerful strategic advantage in the pulp and paper industry. The new economy and some old sloth combined to blow it away. We didn't keep pace with reinvestments, specifically into environmentally safer processes. And we didn't move aggressively into recycling—for some very good reasons. Canadian mills are in the wrong place: think, for instance, of a newsprint mill in Pennsylvania, which is within easy access of Philadelphia and New York, versus one in northern Quebec. The Quebecer has to import the old newspapers from Pennsylvania or somewhere else in the United States to northern Quebec, make the paper, and then ship it back. We've got a freight penalty both ways.

The business has changed in other fundamental ways. Consumption of newsprint used to grow between half and two-thirds the rate of GNP. Then in the early 1980s, advertising had a heyday. Newpapers got at least their share of that advertising, and newsprint consumption grew as fast as GNP. Then, by 1987, advertising really cut back—retail, financial, real estate. That kind of advertising is the mainstay of newspapers. Newspapers, after all, aren't an information medium, they're an advertising medium. Owners throw in a little bit of other stuff to keep you happy. So, for the first time in about fifty years, newsprint consumption dropped off materially. In previous recessions it flattened out, but it didn't really take a dive. It has never come back. Linn Macdonald, chief executive of Noranda Forest, says, "I think advertising is on a new path. Most of the industry says that as soon as the cohort of the right age group gets into that reading age you're going to see the readership and circulation jump. I don't think so. Kids today have been brought up on TV; that's where they get their information, and they aren't going to change." Macdonald is probably right. Newspapers are an old economy industry. Few cities have more than one paper. But, as with other industries, newspapers won't disappear, they'll just change. They're already making adjustments. Ownership is concentrating at the same time product is proliferating. Sections are targeted to specific markets, and satellite communications and desktop publishing have revolutionized the printing process. There's spin-off from this phenomenon, too. Adds Macdonald, "I'd be reluctant to invest huge amounts of money in newsprint mills unless I had a very special opportunity to build a very low cost mill, right beside its customers, and could make money even in a difficult market." Special opportunities are around for the guy who sees them. International Paper, Macdonald reminisced, was the last company making tab card stock (remember punch cards?). Everyone else had gone out of the business because it was obviously phasing out. But IP made a potful of money as the last guy making tab cards.

So what's the future for the pulp and paper industry? There will for many years be mills in Canada producing virgin fiber, because you can't recycle everything indefinitely; there has to be some virgin fiber in the mix to "sweeten" it. Likely the pulp business will remain, because pulp is the basic building block for so many grades of paper. Paper will continue to be an advertising medium—direct mail, magazines, particularly the ones that focus narrowly on what the customer wants. The new chief executive at Southam says, "I'm dreaming about you getting a newspaper that's just for you. You don't want real estate, you don't get it. You want a special car section, you get it..." Magazines already do that. You buy a car magazine or *Better Homes & Gardens* because they've got that segmentation. Direct mail does the same thing. The ability of computer systems to determine the probable wants of a particular name on the mailing list is getting better and better. The pulp business is the basic building block for magazine paper and the paper that's used in direct mail advertising, as well as for all business papers.

Some of the changes are unpredictable. Everyone thought that computers would reduce the use of office paper. But now we're getting one computer printout instead of letting the typewriter type out many copies. Then we run off twenty copies of that printout on heavier paper (more expensive, less environmentally friendly). Communication papers such as office stationery will probably be around for a long time. Studies show that this is one way to present your company with some impact. You run a risk by using substandard or

shoddy product, since your letter is the only thing new contacts know about your company until they meet you.

In the building materials area, technology is already changing the industry. Standard dimension lumber—two-by-fours,
two-by-sixes and so on—is already in some companies giving
way to special composite materials engineered out of wastewood
or wood that isn't good enough to make lumber out of. Plywood
is being replaced by more sophisticated products made with
cheaper wood, but which do a superior job. Where plywood
used to be hidden in the construction, these new products have
better structural integrity and are decorative—they're being
used for visual effects.

Another big challenge of the future for the goods-producing industries is marketing their products. Many have been
content to concentrate on making things, not actively selling
them. That orientation removes them just enough from the
customer so that they are not as well tuned in to where things
are going and how the economy and business are shifting.
When companies focus on producing, they tend to build another mill or another factory to make the same product as the
last one. Global competition has finished that—that era's
come to an end. Successful businesses need to be market ori-
ented. They need to know in advance what the customer wants.
And then supply it.

Overall, to meet the challenges of the future, it's clear
Canadians need a new direction, one that is more market ori-
ented, more aware of products, distribution systems and the
needs of specific market niches. Expansion in North America
lies more in the United States than in Canada. And Canada's
educational structures and infrastructure will need to help
Canadians achieve those goals.

Meanwhile, one point stands out. If business is flat, it means
the industry is not making enough products people want to
buy. That's not cyclical. The situation won't change by itself,
or with governments stimulating the economy. If a company

wants to prosper, it just has to come up with a great product and get it to market. As more and more businesses operate according to the new economic laws of information production, the less cyclical behavior there'll be in the economic base.

And One More Thing...

The maturing of the baby boomers combined with the trend to longer and healthier post-retirement years is about to do for the volunteer sector what the baby boomers first did for hula hoops: make volunteering the hottest thing on the planet. As already mentioned, volunteering in Canada contributes more to the economy than mines and forestry, utilities and communications —around $12 billion a year, according to a federal government study. The sectors that chiefly benefit from volunteer work are culture, crafts, adventure tourism and community-based environmental industries.

But perhaps the most interesting thing about the volunteer sector in an age of shattering economic paradigms is that it represents a nonmarket alternative that generally enhances quality over what the market provides. We all learned back in Economics 101 that supply and demand insured the best quality for the least price. But volunteered services come free, and often with a commitment money can't buy. Richard Titmuss, a British social scientist, drew attention to that fact in the 1970s in a book called *The Gift Relationship*. In it, Titmuss compared commercially available blood with donated blood to show that the act of giving contains a value-enhancing component that market-supplied products generally don't. True, today, with continous quality improvements the management rage, the contrast might not be so clear. But when you look at how continuous quality improvement works, it's the nonmarket aspects of team building and empowerment that make the difference between success and failure—in essence a matter of the gift of trust.

So when we're talking agents of change for the 1990s and beyond, look out: we're about to be hit by tough-minded, highly trained, management-smart volunteers who are really going to make things work in the areas they care about. And that covers the waterfront.

Five

Agriculture in an Information Economy

What concerns me is not the way things are,
but rather the way people think things are.
—Epictetus

CROP FAILURE! AFRICA'S the only place left where people perish when the harvest fails. That's almost entirely because of the way the world organizes farming. And the way the world organizes farming came with the emergence of industrial society and the horrible world wars that accompanied that shift.

There are a couple of reasons agriculture is a topic here. First, completing the shift from an industrially based economy to an information one is going to involve our very vocal farm communities. Second, looking at the way agriculture is practised is instructive for spotlighting the mistakes from which we must finally learn, and the institutional walls in need of Joshua's horn, if today's transition is to develop more smoothly than it's done to date.

In its natural state, farming is the struggle of faith against uncertainty. The uncertainties facing farmers—from weather, crop disease, competition and so on—are so great that there would be many fewer farmers without additional guarantees.

Yet without the farmer to produce the grains, vegetables and animals for reliable food supplies, all advanced societies would cease to exist. Not surprisingly, therefore, farmers and everyone else in agribusiness turn to their communities—and government as agent of the communities—to reduce uncertainty.

Canadian agricultural programs are designed to insure that the returns are sufficiently assured that a steady supply of affordable farm products is available. The philosophy behind the United States price support programs and the European Community Common Agricultural Policy is similar—to ensure adequate food supplies by taking some of the uncertainty out of the return.

The problems arise when society makes the assumption that the uncertainties facing farmers are somehow different from the uncertainties facing other small producers in the global marketplace. They're not, but we've assumed they are. And having done that, we've tied farmers' assistance to the crops they produce. Farmers don't get unemployment insurance. They get price stabilization programs and crop insurance and special emergency assistance.

The drawback to this kind of risk reduction is that it locks in the status quo. It adds to the cost of change instead of promoting adjustment to world conditions. As we're seeing worldwide, this kind of fundamental policy error is more than a theoretical point. It's potentially disastrous. For what happens when everybody is insured against uncertainty by locking in payment for output that can't be sold? Instead of undercommitment of resources, we have overcommitment. These particular attempts to stabilize domestic farm economies encounter the paradox of global economies. The paradox is that efforts to stabilize locally, destabilize the international economy. The issue gets worse when the big players start playing subsidy chicken. Prices plunge below cost, and those without bottomless pockets face bankruptcy and exit. As is so often the case with economics, what seems desirable to individuals ends up making everybody worse off. National programs to stabilize returns produce international results that destabilize returns more than ever.

This is hardly the first time these mistakes have been made. World War I was the single most important reason more North and South American land came into food production. And when Europe recovered and put its farmland back into production, the combined huge acreages and vast volumes pushed down commodity prices. That led government after government to put up trade barriers. The trade barriers ultimately pushed the international economy down into the Great Depression. Now we're seeing the same daffy logic at work in the beggar-thy-neighbor subsidies that are intended to shore up the policy that ties farmers' assistance to the crops they produce. At $80 billion a year, Europe's Common Agriculture Policy is probably the worst offender. To make matters worse, as we've seen in recent months, western Europe is even trying to block imports from eastern Europe—the same eastern European countries that so badly need hard currency to help kick start their own economies, deranged as they are by fifty years or so of central planning.

In the mid 1980s European subsidies and dumping in third-country markets led to retaliation by other producers, chiefly the United States. Farm commodity prices had, inevitably, to collapse on world markets. And, of course, we now also have a historic economic restructuring, which isn't helped by huge distortions in the price structure of agricultural products.

So here we are, the most expensively educated generation in history, and we haven't yet learned the disastrous lessons protectionism has to teach us. As a result, agriculture is the only major commodity in international circulation that's not governed by normal trading rules. Subsidies for farmers and barriers to food imports reign in Europe and North America, and even in Japan—although Japan is not a food exporter. Because of those barriers to trade, excess food supplies are dumped

in developing countries—a situation that effectively prevents
the modernization of African agriculture (along with a host of
other causes, such as crooked governments and no official
system of financial credit). When you look at Africa today, you
can see where protectionism leads: death, destruction and
economic failure. When you look at the rest of the world, you
can see how trade barriers distort markets and render them
less efficient.

The transition from an agriculture-based economy to an industrial one in the last century was a much bigger social, economic
and cultural shift than we've seen to date in this transition. When
you think that the number of agriculture workers dropped from
seventy percent of the population to less than four percent, you
come to realize that almost the entire population of North America
lost their jobs. Painful as that might have been, the shift was
accompanied by a huge surge in productivity as labor moved
from less productive land into tremendously productive factories. And, thanks to many new technologies, a tiny fraction of
the labor force is now able to produce more than the much larger labor force of even sixty years ago.

It's no exaggeration to say that everything that's wrong
with farming today can be traced to government interference
in the market—the wrong kind of interference, based on nostalgia instead of on a hardheaded evaluation of what's what.
So instead of helpful, market-wise intervention, we have programs designed to keep market logic at bay. That results in
keeping inefficient, less productive land in production worldwide. More than that, the present situation is unsustainable.
Whatever the shock of liberalization, that shock amounts to the
collection of a long overdue bill on misused national resources.

Agriculture and World Trading Rules

Half a century ago, when the post-war international order and
the world's trading treaty, the General Agreement on Tariffs

and Trade (GATT), was written, the United States insisted that the GATT exclude agricultural products. Now, if trade liberalization is to continue, the Uruguay Round negotiators are having to correct this error.

Here's a quick tiptoe through the tulips of world trade talks. First, they're called rounds. Second, there have been half a dozen or more rounds since 1946 (the Great Depression and World War II actually convinced a few people that protectionism was not politically correct). The one we're in now is the Uruguay Round. This one was supposed to be finished in 1991, but American and European trade negotiators were still stumped, not on how to bring agriculture into the deal, but how to bring it in without jeopardizing the cushy jobs of their political masters at home. Thinking and acting globally has not yet been reconciled with voters turfing out politicians locally.

Anyway, the talks didn't collapse. They didn't collapse because business pressure was brought to bear on many governments around the world to liberalize trade. Business wants trade liberalization because its new processes need (and needed even in the early 1980s) a global playing field. Even though agricultural interests, worldwide, are powerful (farmers' votes weigh disproportionately at the polls), they aren't as powerful as the need of manufacturers and service providers for free trade. So negotiations continued among the experts, and finally a deal on agriculture is in sight.

Canada's been in a tough position in these talks because we're both a major exporter (and thus need trade liberalization) as well as a major user of supply management programs. The deal that will eventually be made will phase out, sometime in the next century, supply management programs so that domestic producers make the same adjustments as everyone else: meet the global competition or close. But you needn't cry for farmers; during the phaseout, they'll be operating behind tariff walls of 150% or more. You may, as a consumer, want to ask why that is so.

The new GATT rules for farming will bring normal international trading rules into the farming sector—especially the changes that weaken or eliminate Article XI, the section of the GATT treaty that permits the establishment of supply management boards, despite the fact that they restrict international trade. (You'll be fawned on by adoring crowds at cocktail parties with this arcane detail, right?) Actually, it's more accurate to say the new GATT rules will complete the work of bringing those changes into the food sector, for the main beneficiaries will be food processing companies, including Canadian ones.

The details of the new GATT agreement have yet to be released. But whatever it says, once food follows normal trading rules, Canadian food packagers, processors and distributors will benefit, and all but the most knowledge-intensive dairy and poultry farmers will not. Ontario and Quebec together generate about sixty percent of the poultry business in Canada. Poultry supply is managed by government decree. Canada's heaviest commitment to supply managed dairy farms is in Quebec. ("Supply management" programs are essentially government controlled or approved monopolies aimed at increasing incomes of producers, and stabilizing domestic markets and prices. Imports of commodities whose supply is managed are either blocked entirely or quantitatively limited. Wheat, barley, oats and their products, all dairy products, eggs, chickens and turkeys are directly supply managed. In addition, many processed and fresh food products are protected.) Anything that poses problems for Quebec is never simple because of our political dichotomy. With Quebec generating half the $3 billion dairy products revenue, it poses big problems.

All Power Corrupts, But We Need Electricity

What we're seeing is the shifting of agriculture from the industrial to the information age. It's taking on the same organizational forms that other productive enterprises are adopting—strategic cooperation and the exploitation of niche markets, such as local cheeses, or alliances with food processing companies to develop new, specialty-based food products. Even with supply management programs in place, dairy farms are currently closing at the rate of five to six percent a year. Operations are consolidating. Larger operations can use more advanced management techniques. Because of the enormous transition that agriculture has already survived, history suggests that, despite the doom-ridden forecasts of many eastern Canadian farmers, successful adjustment is by far the most probable outcome. When able to respond to market forces, agriculture evolves to keep pace with changes in society.

As North America industrialized, so did rural Canada and the United States, as exemplified by the spread of electrification and mechanization to rural areas. (When asked for his definition of socialism sometime after he had consolidated his power in the new Soviet state, Lenin is reputed to have replied, "Electrification, electrification, electrification," showing the compelling power of factory metaphors in an industrializing society).

Now that North America has evolved into an information-driven society, so too has farming. Today's farm is a globally sensitive, high-tech, capital intensive enterprise. Overall, because the market has encouraged these shifts to occur, agriculture is a huge North American success story. George Richardson, head of one of Canada's largest agribusiness and financial-services conglomerates, talks about delivering grain, 1990s-style: "Even a country elevator today is operated by computer. In the old days, grain was hauled in by horse and wagon, dumped and elevated; then the car was loaded and weighed back into the hopper, elevated again and put on the car. Now, elevators are computer controlled: the elevator manager comes in in the morning, puts a disk into the PC, types in the bins in the elevator he wants to draw the grain from, goes out back and makes sure that the spout is in the hopper car. He operates the elevator with a little remote box. The computer opens the valves and weighs out the right amount and shuts off when it's finished. The net result in the grain trade is that computerization's been a tremendous help. Same as in the investment industry."

Glenn Stith, head of Winnipeg-based Monsanto Agricultural Chemicals, says western farmers are learning how to make money with wheat at $2 a bushel. "They're getting out from under their $200,000 four-wheel-drive tractors and the maintenance burden, and they're moving to zero tillage. No more nice neat furrows, but they're developing some real smart, knowledge-intensive farming techniques, and they're surviving." In the process, environmentally sound agriculture is coming into its own.

Is There a Role for Public Policy?

The way to fix the distortions caused by government interference in the market for many agricultural products, is to treat agriculture like other business. The problem is not that farmers get government assistance. Everyone gets some kind of government assistance, whether it's help with education, unemployment insurance, publicly subsidized training programs, job counseling or whatever. It doesn't all destabilize world markets. The problem is that agricultural programs are different from the other kinds of individual assistance programs because they're coupled to particular outputs. That's where the instability comes from.

In an interdependent world, we're all connected, like it or not. And we should devise programs to help people respond accordingly: that is, with flexibility and intelligence, not stubborn resistance to the inevitable. For instance, subsidies not only encourage farmers to produce more of the products being subsidized, they also make it more difficult to see market signals. For example, American farmers last year left substantial demand for canola unfilled because, in effect, the United States government paid them to ignore demand for that product. And demand for the stuff is going up because canola makes a low saturated-fat cooking oil. Frito-Lay wants it to make more chips. Procter & Gamble wants to add it to Crisco. Food processing giant Archer Daniel-Midlands is going to try making up the shortfall from southern production. But seeds for that climate have not yet been perfected. Should Canadian farmers be increasing Canadian canola production, despite some Canadian Wheat Board programs that seem to be signaling no? Ironically, high prices were not enough to persuade U.S. farmers to grow more beef in 1992. The United States beef herd stayed near the thirty-year low point it hit in the mid-1980s. Flexibility and the ability to adjust rapidly to changes in demand are what's required for success in the world economy in other sectors. Agriculture's no different.

Yet our subsidy structures inhibit the kinds of flexibility survival requires. For they continue to link what amounts to income support to specific crop output. For some time now, policy analysts have recommended that this support should be uncoupled from specific crop support, just the way the rest of the country gets unemployment insurance payments while they look for other jobs, if necessary—not just a replica of the ones they lost. Indeed, with two-income families, including some off-farm employment, it looks as if the family farm will continue to survive.

There's nothing unique about the family farm situation. If you think about the family farm as a small business, you'll understand why the odds are good that it will survive. Global markets encourage small business in all sectors. For the competitive pressures facing large companies mean that more than before they have to "outsource"—buying or renting their inputs from the cheapest, most efficient source, instead of making them, as they used to. And they buy increasingly from small suppliers.

Nostalgia is a poor guide to appropriate policy. The communications revolutions, the shift to personal computers, the emergence of sophisticated programming and engineering software to run on them means that anyone who really wants to can be a CEO with an ocean of information available. The prospects were never brighter for the small producer, whether industrial or agricultural. It's not the global economy that's putting small farmers at a disadvantage. Rather, the current subsidy and assistance programs favor uneconomic production. Our agricultural and nonagricultural assistance programs have failed to converge the way the agricultural and manufacturing sectors have in our economy. We need to separate agricultural support from specific commodities, just as we separate income maintenance programs from specific activities for the rest of society.

If the world shifts to straight income insurance for farmers, the added flexibility, combined with easily accessible market intelligence, will give Canadians a sizable advantage. But we have to change our thinking to take advantage. That's the hardest part.

Six

Where Does Real Estate Fit In?

I go downtown every day, work ten or twelve
hours, come home tired in the evening. My
house has just sat quietly all day—but it's
made more money than I have.
—Hugh Segal, Toronto resident, circa 1988

PEOPLE CONSTANTLY ASK, "What's driving this restructuring of the economy? Where can we see it happening?"

Let's take a look at real estate. Why, after dozens of years of being able to count on your house to provide you with a good part of your retirement income, can you not count on it any more? How is it possible that Olympia & York, the world's biggest real estate development company, was in bankruptcy court for protection from its creditors? The fact is, the old solid growth chestnut—the land we own, our property—is unlikely in our lifetime to be the kind of investment it has been for the past forty years.

The reasons? A global, information-based economy is witheringly competitive, pushing prices down, moving us from half a century of more or less inflation to no inflation and deflation. A global information-based economy is not bound so closely to places. Cities are the product of the 1880s industrial revolution and the invention of mass

production. Now, we're into mass customization and service, which don't necessarily need to be located where
they've been before. Our demographic pattern, which is
fixed for several decades at least, our life-style changes
and the reorganization of business establishments suggest
a different role for cities and therefore have an effect on
real estate values.

Among the changes is a significant shift away from inflation
gains. Residential and commercial properties have benefited for
forty-five years from inflationary price rises, first in the generally inflationary 1960s, as Canada urbanized rapidly after
World War II, and more specifically after the tax reform of
1971 exempted owner-occupied homes from capital gains tax.
Now technology and demographics ensure the reversal of
developments that began in the early 1960s, got out of control between the mid-1960s and mid-1970s and took two recessions to subdue, the recession of 1981–82 and that of 1990–91.
It's not just the outsiders who are saying this. William Dimma
is the chairman of Royal Lepage, Canada's largest real estate
seller. He says, "We'll have almost no commercial, meaning
office, building, other than that already committed, until the end
of this century." He acknowledges that there'll be some regional variations. Vancouver, for example, has barely been touched
by the general decline of real estate values. But in Toronto,
the undisputed where-it's-happening capital of Canada for the
past fifty years, Dimma anticipates "no buildings of any consequence" being built in the foreseeable future, aside from the
ones that have been started.

What a difference a new paradigm makes. But think about
it. North America—and Canada in particular—has been urban-
izing for the past hundred years, creating a new-housing and
commercial heaven. But two phenomena combine to make
us wonder how this trend fits with the new economy. The two
phenomena are demographics and the shift to an information
and service-based economy.

The days of large-scale housing starts is over as the baby boom generation ages and its bulk moves up the demographic charts like a bulge in the belly of a snake. The annual growth in Canadian households to the turn of the century will slow to only half the rate experienced in the past three decades. Linn Macdonald, president and CEO, Noranda Forest, says, "Demographics alone are going to mean we're probably never going to see two million plus housing starts again in the U.S. as was the case a few years ago. Last year [1991], starts were the lowest in fifty years. It'll get better than that, but maybe a million and a half housing starts are going to be the upper limit". First-time home buyers traditionally are households headed by people aged twenty-five to thirty-four. We'll have almost two hundred thousand fewer people in that age group by 1996. Clearly, the total demand for housing units has to decline. Says Dimma, "The baby boomlets, or the last of the baby boomers, are just now passing through the snake. That's the last bulge in the snake, and it will help the housing market through about 1995 or 1996." What Dimma means is that the twenty-five-percent average decline in house prices across the country in the last few years would be a lot higher if it weren't for the last of the boomers still looking for a starter home. After 1996, no boomers will be in the market for a first home. The "shadow" baby boom, that is, an uptick in Canada's birthrate because of the huge number of boomers deciding to have a child, was evident in 1988. They'll be old enough to be first-time home buyers in 2013.

The conclusion for housing demand is clear. Total demand for housing units will continue to decrease. Demand for lower priced starter homes will decrease most, while demand for higher quality, customised, single, detached or low-maintenance housing will increase dramatically. By the same token, recreational properties may be entering a golden age, because the average home owner pays off the mortgage at the age of forty-four. Suddenly, there will be a lot more disposable income. The

average baby boomer, say, those born around 1956 or 1957, will
be forty-four sometime near the turn of the century. So, it's possible the demand for recreational properties may also be strong.

Clearly, housing developers have to shift their emphasis
from building a large quantity of lower-value starter homes to
renovating existing stock or in-filling (tearing down what's
there and building higher quality "trade-up" homes.) Failing
this shift, there's likely to be a staggering mismatch of supply
and demand.

Policy makers will have to turn their attention away from
universal, national or even provincial policies and toward narrowly focused policies that target narrowly focused problems.
They'll have to start cooperating with other policy makers to
deal with obstacles to solutions—for example, municipal zon-
ing rigidities that prevent rather than facilitate alternative land
use and development.

As for the homes that already exist, their prices will come
down more or less permanently for some other social and
economic forces. Joel Garreau, senior writer at the *Washington
Post*, recently coined the phrase "edge cities" to describe
what's happening to our cities. They are being restructured
into multicentered focal points—interdependent clusters of
businesses, offices, homes, commercial and industrial space.
As a result, metropolitan regions have expanded dramatically, while central downtowns' shares of regional office
space and economic activity have declined. Look at downtown
Toronto, Montreal, Winnipeg, Regina (as well as Los Angeles,
Miami, Boston and Philadelphia) to see it yourself. Says
Garreau, "Edge cities are the culmination of a generation of
individual American value decisions about the best ways to
live, work and play—about how to create home... Edge cities
acculturate immigrants, provide child care, offer safety. That's
why they're the crucible of America's urban future." Estimates
are that there's been enough commercial space built in
Canada's downtown cores to satisfy traditional demand for

the next seven to ten years. With small enterprises—those with fewer than a hundred employees—creating most of the new jobs, and with fully equipped office satellites springing up in the exurbs, it may take even longer to fill the space that's already been built. Or it may be that the space, built for commercial enterprise, will be transformed into multifunctional space—living areas on the lower levels, with access to the street, school and office on the upper levels. The point is that the new economy changes the function of real estate and property, and its value, and therefore its price.

We all intuitively understand that the information revolution is threatening many communities whose major or only employers are in businesses that have become or will become obsolete. Nuala Beck, economic consultant, says her research shows that "if you're employed in that old economy, you stand a better than fifty percent chance that you'll lose your job. So a lot of communities will see their hopes and dreams go down the tubes... unless they do something about it."

Of course, the shift away from housing has lots of fallout. The demographic changes also imply a shift away from the business that supplies residential housing with most of its building supplies—the forest products sector. In addition, the real estate sector is almost totally financed by the banks. Allan Taylor, president and CEO, Royal Bank of Canada, Canada's largest bank, says, "Take a look at what's happened to the banks... and not just the American banks. The past two years' bank earnings have been devastated because of real estate. No doubt there's been a meltdown of value in real estate. When it's a problem for them, it very quickly becomes a problem for the lenders—because we've loaned on a certain understanding of value."

There's also an upside to the real estate situation. The fact that real estate is no longer the sure bet it once was means that more capital will be directed into investment in the real source of economic wealth: invention and innovation. This shift is going to take time, since investors, whether individual or institutional, have to figure out how to make money investing in brains, just as they had to figure out how to make money in inflationary times, and how to make money in industrial endeavors. Over time, Canadian banks will become more knowledgeable about knowledge-based business. The fact that Microsoft is now valued at about the same as General Motors—a valuation that Canadian banks have not up to now been equipped to make—is another indication that, however much they lag the pack, Canadian banks will be dragged along by sheer force of circumstance.

Does It Matter Where You Live?

Not as much as it used to. There's the story of the laid-off factory worker who together with his wife started a newsletter on how to save money. Its circulation shot up to a hundred thousand, and they employ three people. They happen to live in a small town. YMCA Canada's entrepreneurship program each year helps several thousand Canadians take a business idea from concept to implementation. The ideas are the products of their clients' imaginations, based on individual experience and knowledge. The Y provides the incubator, the coaching, the support. The Y operates in metropolitan areas and in remote regions.

Throughout Canada and the United States, there are a growing number of computer bulletin boards—somewhere in the tens of thousands—that earn steady and respectable returns for the system operators who run them. All it takes is about $5,000 of computer equipment and a good idea. If it serves the right niche and those calling in can pay with a credit card, you've got a business with a global potential. There are more than 22 million homeworkers in the United States and Canada—most taking advantage of their knowledge to make a living. The boards themselves deal with anything with a worldwide following: could be a compendium of files on tropical fish, with a little space for people to chat and leave messages.The fact is, with a computer you can communicate around the world for the price of a local call (although today, in its infancy, it can take some doing). But a new business doesn't have to be computer-based; it could be a direct mail business or a fax-based business. The thing is, it's a personal, direct link with the outside world that can't be controlled by anyone else. When you think about creating value, remember you're doing it in a world economy—not just a provincial or a local one.

The new corporate organizational forms promise to make suburbs into global hubs just as the downtowns were for an industrial economy. Richard Lipsey, senior fellow, Institute for Advanced Research, points out that as the corporation becomes a looser structure of semi-independent bodies, "there's more local provision of services to the corporation— things that used to be done centrally are being done by three independent companies operating in small units." That's typical of what's happening everywhere. It's bringing back to the suburb the life that deserted it when everyone was off at work. We're changing our cities, towns and villages to integrate living and working much more.

As our information society matures, these shifts will be pronounced. Cities will be more important than countries, with certain cities acting as international information nodes. Some experts call them "information service stations." Transforming, rerouting, redirecting information is very profitable. Singapore, for example, has already achieved this. It has the cheapest phone rates in the region. So Singapore has attracted the most phone traffic. It has the most consistently profitable phone company in the world. The engineering demands of keeping the system at the leading edge has improved its whole telecommunications sector.

Singapore is also a shipping hub and a trading hub. Its telecommunications base allows it to leverage those strengths by creating the largest shipping data base in the world. According to the experts in this field (such as Stan Davis and Bill Davidson, or Professor Jagdish Seth), Singapore offers one pattern other cities might want to follow. Possibly we'll see the world's cities arranged hierarchically according to their volume of telecommunications traffic. The richest cities will be those that service the most traffic. They'll be the world's information hubs. Other, lesser cities will feed into those hubs. They'll be dominated by single telecommunications companies. The telecommunications companies will have suppliers of every kind of information imaginable. The delivery hardware will be yours to choose. The technology will be based on open architectures, as computers are today. In other words, the system will be designed to take advantage of a unique characteristic of network-related intellectual property: its value increases the more people use it. So the technology will permit the ready use of equipment from other suppliers. This will create a fabulous business for software suppliers.

The information suppliers will include theater companies, universities, photographers, newspapers, think tanks, writers, photographers, banks—all of whom will sell their products to as many hubs as will buy. Differences between world class and local suppliers will be reflected in the price. All this will have a huge impact on education. For example, expensive schools will use more world class educational services than other schools which will supplement their smaller range with more locally produced content.

The hardware suppliers will likely be independent of the telephone company operators. But there'll be lots of interrelations and alliances creating local bargains that jobbers will arbitrage worldwide. The main competition to the hub cities will come from geocentric satellite services that cover regions. The whole thing will be consumer driven. International data transfer will be a major link between countries.

This is a major opportunity for Canada but one that our current regulatory picture prevents us from capturing. While geographic location means much less than it used to, time and opportunity mean as much as they ever did. And these mind-boggling changes are only just emerging. Canada, standing midway between the two fastest growing regions in the world and atop the third, could be the central transpacific, transatlantic and transpolar link between Europe, North America and Asia—if we had a forward-looking telecommunications policy. For a city that was looking for a growth strategy, this could be it: become the Singapore of North America. Unfortunately, Canada doesn't have a good telecommunications policy. Nor does it seem likely, given the way our inter-regional bargaining works, that we'll get one any time soon. More institutional drag.

This is just one example. But it fits the argument here, that the market is making the shifts society needs—out of inflation-driven profits in real estate toward knowledge-based industries.

Seven

Manufacturing, New Style

If you don't ask "why this?" often enough,
somebody will ask "why you?"
                              —Tom Hirshfield

CANADA HAS LOST 350,000 jobs in the past few years, most of
them permanently. The unemployment rate is significantly
double digit, with no indication that it's likely to recede.
What's to blame? Machines? Robots replacing workers?
Computers replacing clerks and middle managers? There's
something to this. But it's misleading. In fact, two things
increase ouputs while closing down job openings—globalization and competition.

Globalization means your market's no longer at home. It's
a narrow niche somewhere over the horizon. Your product
sells in, say, twenty to seventy countries worldwide. So you
don't have to depend on full employment at home for a good
market. There's enough employment worldwide to create
enough demand for your global product—although not necessarily for a national product. That demand pulls output
upward, although slowly.

The second force closing down jobs is competition. Global
competition is witheringly intense. It's based on time—chiefly
the time it takes to get your product to market. To thrive in a

global economy, you have to get your product out to as much of your niche as you can. You need to build volume fast as a defense against the competition. Because the competition will copy your product and have a rival in place within two years or less.

The future of production work is totally linked to progress in "informatics"—computerization. In Japan, new plans for what they call "intelligent manufacturing systems" (IMS) call for factories to run like sushi bars: you arrive at the showroom, point to the combination of product modules you want, and three days later you can come and pick up your more or less personalized automobile. For less complicated products, for example bicycles and bathing suits, that kind of service exists now, but on a same-day basis. That's right. If you go to an advanced bicycle shop, they will measure you using a computer hooked into the production system, and after some time has passed, voila! a tailor-made bicycle. Similar IMS factory systems are being proposed in the United States, where they're known as "agile manufacturing."

It's interesting to compare the pressures behind these developments in Japan and the United States, because they reflect the future of manufacturing and labor: not enough qualified people.

In Japan, it's demographics. The population is aging. And the capacity of the country to absorb foreigners or women onto the factory floor, they recognize, is limited. So they're looking to machines to leverage the few available workers.

In the United States, the pressures are rather different: not the shortage of people, but the shortage of qualified workers! A segment of manufacturing is, in effect, suggesting that even with a turnaround, the United States education system would not be able to deliver the number of qualified workers advanced manufacturing requires.

In Canada, despite the fact we're considered by the UN as the best country in the world in which to live, our education

system still hasn't caught up with the change in production—
the shift from industrial worker to knowledge worker. We still
have a national high-school dropout rate of around thirty percent, and the number of industrial workers unable to understand
written instruction of the difficulty level of a bus schedule is
around forty percent.

Knowledge work will spread by the turn of the century,
and the education system may have caught up. But right now
Canada as a whole is losing the game. For the past ten years,
our exports, in real terms, have grown only half as fast as our
imports. In other words, our appetite for the international
products of others is running far ahead of others' appetites
for our own. Our merchandise trade growth is increasing more
slowly than domestic growth. If our goods-producing sectors
were successfully internationalizing, merchandise exports
would outpace national growth. But over the same ten years,
total economic growth outpaced trade growth almost two to
one. Between 1980 and 1990, the value of all the goods and
services we produced (our gross domestic product, or GDP)
increased by about thirty-three percent. Merchandise export
growth, on the other hand, increased by only eighteen percent
over the same period, about half the rate of national growth.
When services are included, the situation improves. But in real
terms, over the past ten years, our total export sector growth
has been increasing more slowly than the economy as a whole.

Something similar is happening on the investment side.
We're getting more foreign investment, and foreign investors
are getting into areas other than the traditional ones—natural
resources and heavy manufacturing. But in relation to the
economy as a whole, foreign direct investment—that is, what
economists call investment in "productive facilities" such as
financial services or electronics factories as opposed to investment in things such as bonds—isn't growing much. Foreign-
owned companies operating in Canada are reinvesting their
profits in Canada. But foreign-owned companies operating

in the United States are reinvesting faster there. That means the United States is modernizing faster than we are—fifty percent faster over the past decade.

Mind you, the small business sector, despite the failure rate, is still growing. Global markets encourage small business, as we noted earlier, because bigger companies "outsource" more than they used to. And they buy increasingly from small suppliers, though they put a lot of pressure on those suppliers to ensure that they produce exactly the right component at exactly the right time for its incorporation into the final product. (This is called just-in-time manufacturing.) Japanese companies are leading the pressure for this kind of change, and United States companies are following. Now the key to bringing that revolution to Canada is to improve small companies' access to advanced, computer assisted manufacturing and design technologies, so-called CAD/CAM systems. A recent innovation in this area is industrial extension services. Like agriculture in the 1930s and 1940s, small and medium-sized manufacturing in North America is the recipient of government aid to encourage technology transfer. Throughout the United States, and also in Canada, governments are setting up "technology diffusion centers." These programs are designed to bring universities, local business and government research labs together to provide businesses with the problem-solving, technical assistance they need to upgrade their manufacturing processes. This is not so different from the promotion of rural electrification and scientific farming that began during the Great Depression—much of which still survives in the United States agriculture extension services and the programs of Agriculture Canada.

But the shift to knowledge work has to be seen as a personal challenge. For as factories themselves become more intelligent and able to run with a minimum of people, the opportunities for outside suppliers and other local small business people will increase. Here's where projects like Junior

Achievement school programs and the YMCA enterprise centers come in. The former let children know there are other work categories besides "employee" by teaching entrepreneurship and business ownership. The latter give typical new knowledge workers the opportunity to put their ideas and knowledge to work with the maximum scope for success. The typical Canadian worker will do well to the degree that he or she participates in the global knowledge economy, adding value of some sort to the global circulation of information. Workers who can add value can do so on their own or as part of a larger organization. Workers and companies will thus gradually evolve into de facto partnerships. Which raises the question: what about the individual workers who are not in a position to transform knowledge, to add value? They will be least favored by a knowledge-based society. Indeed, manufacturing is about to evolve to the point that it will not to have to deal with these people.

The best we can do to keep the numbers low is by entrepreneurship training and by emphasizing that it's never too late to upgrade one's training to become a knowledge worker. If we do that, we can go a long way towards ensuring a highly productive, interesting life, full of achievement, for everyone. Nuala Beck's formula for success: "Hitch your wagon to the right horse. There are whole industries out there that are growing and thriving... that are the new economy... that are expanding. That's where the jobs and the future are going to be."

There's nothing complicated about any of this. The fact is that no tree grows to the sky, no industry grows forever, and no product line lasts a thousand years. New industries replace old industries as the engines of growth. Beck cautions municipalities trying to work their magic in economic development: "The last thing you want is to go after and attract an employer only to find that he spends the next five years downsizing on you. It's a lot smarter, and more effective, to know the new economy companies which, when you bring them into your town, will be expanding and growing and creating a future for your community."

Where are Knowledge Workers Heading?

A buzzword among enlightened global competitors is "strategic alliance," and it spins off to knowledge workers, too. Strategic alliances are different from mergers and acquisitions, although the most successful strategic alliances involve some exchange of stock. The key idea here is that new products have to get to market quickly—before the competition can duplicate them. Few companies—not even the largest—can afford to maintain by themselves all the distribution channels a global product launch requires. Especially when real interest rates remain high and there are other costs, such as rigidity and inefficiency, if you get too big.

So companies are prowling for partners—other companies with which to swap products and market access, through licensing and other techniques. These company arrangements translate into relationships among corporation employees that are akin to large families with lots of cousins. They also result in a lot more employee autonomy and visibility. A successful product and the team responsible will go around the network, advising on how to launch the product, how to service it, and so on. The full implications of networking strategies have not yet emerged. Clearly, companies that compete on some levels also cooperate on others. The point for employees is simply this: these arrangements decrease risk, and not only for products. Knowledge workers in linked companies can become knowledge workers in each company.

Where Are Manufactories Headed?

So far, this book has had a lot to say about sectoral shifts out of traditional manufacturing, as well as the changing

economics of manufacturing as a result of its computerization. But it hasn't yet explored what may be the most interesting, if the subtlest, shift of all—the shift in the nature of
manufacturing. This shift is so subtle and so stunning that the
traditional arguments about sectoral shifts become blurred
beyond recognition.

What is manufacturing? Say it's metal stamping, for example. The actual stamping is only part of the process. The tem-
plate governing the stamping is also a part. Say it's welding.
The programming of the robot that does the welds, the paint-
ing and some of the assembly work are also part of the process. Yet these designing, programming jobs are normally
considered something other than manufacture, namely services.

Remember the Salomon Brothers and other investment
dealers? They used computers to reformulate credit instruments for international capital markets. The raw material came
from borrowers of a certain credit rating, such as government
or corporate bonds. But then the traders got to work on them,
stripped off their coupons for sale as a separate income stream
to investors prepared to pay for an income investment, and
sold the coupon-stripped bond to other customers who wanted to invest for capital gains. There were as many variations
on these themes as there were customers, as the factory computers transformed raw credit into investment portfolios customized to match the high-reward or minimum-risk strategies
of the investors.

The same logic applies in other sectors we typically think of
as services. They have now become manufacturers. For instance,
think about a school, college or university that "manufactures"
its courses. What if those courses are sold as "courseware" on
a national and international scale? This is happening. At the
Open Learning Agency in Burnaby, British Columbia, for example, they sell their own stock (it doesn't matter whether the
stock is a widget or a course) as is, or sell it as modules to be
reassembled by the buyer (client, employer), or they seek other

materials they can broker, or they custom-make product on demand. Lucille Pacey, vice president of the agency, says, "We produce our courseware via electronic publishing, so we've all got computer terminals on our desks; we can transfer files quickly, and print electronically."

Producing educational materials has become new economy manufacturing. Like old economy manufacturing, educators now have factory space problems. The Open Learning Agency just built a new building. In doing so, its managers had to ensure that the building would grow with them, and that they had the degree of flexibility they needed to focus on their business and the kind of work they do. The entire building was therefore built in modules so they can add to it and extend their communication networks as the technology catches up to what they want to do. Walking through the building, you can see that the wiring is easily accessible; the computer system has a fiber network, the wings have fiber loops, and connecting them is easy.

The agency itself is driven by the use of technology. Pacey says, "Our boardroom and presentation room have been set up to demonstrate to our clients that using technology is simply not a problem. Say I want to make a presentation, and that in it I want to do some graphic stuff using the computer. I want to use a little bit of videotape and maybe some of it is on VHS, some of it on Beta. Maybe I want to download something right off the satellite and bring it here so that people could see what we're doing live. Or broker in some programming. And if I really want to be slick, maybe use a little bit of music to get people's attention. ... We can work with slides, we can work with video, we can work with any combination of that. It also allows us to bring full video conferences into this presentation room, so if we want to talk to people any place else in the province or around the world, we can do that kind of connection and linkage through here. So the entire building allows us to do work in one piece of the building and actually transport it via our fiber system and our cabling system into another room for participants to be involved in it. ... We practice what we preach. And we don't force people to start thinking about different ways of working unless we can actually demonstrate that we can do it."

Then there's the way Corel Systems works. Corel is a software company, founded by Mike Cowpland after he departed from Mitel. The average age of people who work at Corel is about thirty. (Cowpland, who's in his mid-forties, says they have "a few experienced people like myself around.") Cowpland decided to put everything and everybody in one building, even though they sell in about fifty countries. "The nice thing is," he says, "because we're all in one spot, we can use the experience and spread it around quite rapidly, which is another key to the company." Corel works by partnering with other groups elsewhere for the distribution and manufacturing and other things. "That way we can keep this like a beehive of intense communication. Even our sales people in California reside here in Ottawa. So they go out for their ten-day swings, then they come back and get reboosted and energized and retrained on a kind of weekly or monthly basis, not once a year. Because that would be out of date."

What we saw a generation ago was the shift from agriculture to manufacturing and the transformation of agriculture into something like manufacture. Now we're witnessing a shift from manufacture to services—but services that have information embedded in them and allow them to behave like goods. They can be manufactured, stored, shipped, traded— except that the cost of duplication is trivial, and economies of scope are more important than the economies of scale. As this transformation reconfigures manufacturing, it is also reconfiguring agriculture—to make it more customer driven, more responsive, more specialized, and to create niche markets where once mass markets were king.

It's Not the Principle of the Thing, It's the Money

One of the most difficult issues in the transition is money. It's difficult for people with it, and it's difficult for people without it. It's one thing to want to invest $1,000, $10,000, or even $100,000 in the Canadian market. But with only sixty-nine separate corporations operating in Canada today, how do you manage, say, a $1 billion-plus portfolio? Kim Shannon, equity manager at Royal Insurance, says, "It's not easy. There are well over a hundred companies listed on the Toronto Exchange, but McDonald's and Ford don't really trade here, and you have to take out the Bronfmans' and Reichmans' holdings. ... by the time you subtract them all, there's not a lot of selection." As for investing in smaller new economy companies, there's even less chance it will happen. Shannon says her "normal-sized" investment is $20 million. "That could be the entire market capitalization of a small start-up company, and we don't want to own more than ten percent of any company." Her colleague, Alan Westbrook, vice president of investments, says there are two reasons that big institutional investors like the Royal aren't providing venture capital to the new economy. "First, as an insurance company investing our clients' premiums, we have to be very conscious of preserving capital. So we don't want to take big risks. Second, start-up companies in Canada are so small. What we call a large cap company in Canada is really only a medium cap in the States. You'd have to have a basket of them to diminish the risk, and most of them can't absorb more than $1 million." Shannon and Westbrook (and others) think the only way big institutional investors can become involved would be in some kind of pooled fund with an independent manager.

On the receiving end of it, small entrepreneurial businesses marvel at how little the financial institutions understand about knowledge-based business. Bill Cochrane, pediatrician and president of a facilitating venture capital company, says,

"Bankers and investment people are scientifically illiterate, so their due diligence is sometimes inadequate. On the other hand, entrepreneurs don't understand enough about finance, how to raise money, developing a business plan, strategic partnering. ... We need a huge educational effort in these areas." Milton Wong, peripatetic investment counselor and president of M.K. Wong Associates, says we've set up venture capital funds all wrong: "Most venture capital funds have fifty different securities—they expect to win on half and lose on half, They charge two percent in fees. You might as well buy a lottery ticket."

Still, the banking community is front and center in selling mutual funds. They have the money, but there's a problem getting them to move because they have no experience in the right businesses. The financial community has doubled its holdings of government securities over the last year or so, an indication that it is lending neither to traditional borrowers (on whom they've lost money), nor to new, smaller, knowledge-based businesses (which they don't understand). The situation between the bankers and the start-up companies can legitimately be described as "two solitudes." "These guys out of MBA school who come through the investment side just don't link at all to running a business," says Hugh McDiarmid of Stormont Investments. "On the the other hand, the whole high-tech community doesn't understand and appreciate how the capital markets work." Clearly, there's a need for more integration to get the cost of capital down, access to capital up, and to get understanding among the holders of capital and the owners of businesses about the realities of how things work.

Some of it is happening. We need to see the new economy more clearly—and then get our institutions out of the way, unless they can positively help by accelerating these changes. Canada needs these changes to survive. They are like the fundamental shifts in industrial processes that our economies experienced at the end of the last century. Stephen Blank, Director of Canadian Affairs, Americas Society, New York City and a long-time observer of Canada's changing place in North America, says, "The implications of the revolution in the way we make goods are as profound in the 1990s as the implications of the second Industrial Revolution of the 1880s." Until the 1860s, says Blank, production was craft production; it was primarily rural because you had to be close to sources of supply and sources of raw materials. By the 1870s, it suddenly became urban. And sudden change often brings depression. Huge factories were created in the great depression of the 1880s because, as prices collapsed, people had to drive down the cost of production by making bigger and bigger units. What industrial production did then was bring economies of scale into existence. And craft production was essentially finished: it didn't matter how many good pieces you made, they were all the same price. With mechanical industrial production you've got economies of scale. Take, for example, Andrew Carnegie, founder of U.S. Steel. In the space of eight years, he reduced the price of steel bars from $100 a ton to $7 a ton. And with the aid of the legendary financier J.P. Morgan, he consolidated in one company—U.S. Steel—more than a hundred steel companies. A few factories took over the production of a hundred.

Another example, says Blank, is that of J.D. Rockefeller, founder of Standard Oil, which formed the basis of today's global oil industry. He monopolized the production of kerosene, which was the standard fuel of the period, into three refineries. For the whole country.

Another example: Singer Sewing Machines. Singer consolidated its production of sewing machines. It consolidated eighty percent of the world market into two factories, one in England, one in the United States.

Perhaps the ultimate example is Henry Ford. In the fall of 1913, Henry Ford introduced, not the assembly line, but common measurements, so that every piece was made according to the same calibration. That, in turn, meant he was able to design machine tools that could cut hardened steel. Pre-Ford, says Blank, "you made all these pieces and you hardened them and you gave all the pieces to a guy who had a file and a big hammer. And he went off into a room and put all the pieces together." Every car was different. Ford reduced the task turnaround time from five hundred minutes—about ten hours—to seventy minutes. He did that between the fall of 1913 and the spring of 1914. Adding the assembly line was just gilding the lily. But he reduced the task turnaround time to maybe twenty, thirty minutes. Think of that! From five hundred minutes to somewhere around fifty minutes in the space of six months!

The point is, this dizzying pace of change is what's happening to us, right now. Trouble is, we don't have enough of it in the private sector. We still don't have flexible financing. And we still don't have the electronic infrastructure required— that is, a national system that allows anyone to send information in any form over any line.

Eight

News in an Information Age

Oh, no, not another learning experience!
                                    —lapel button

MUCH OF THIS book has argued that the global information economy means an end to business as usual. That's true in spades for the business of news, especially business and political news.

News is not information and never was. Rather, as Walter Lippmann pointed out some seventy years ago, news is a signal that something is happening. "The news" is never the full story. Rather, it's a spur to pursue the facts and develop some information. A more acerbic commentator about the press, and a contemporary of Mr. Lippmann, A.J. Liebling, charged the press with suffering from "guamba" or "meat hunger"—claiming that information in the news had gone the way of the free bar lunch.

The news most of us were brought up on—the signal, not the real thing—is no longer as useful as it once was. In today's information economy, people no longer want news. They want information. They want it in raw streams they can relate to personally and even use by themselves, as unmediated and as unpackaged as possible. This demand is palpable and yet it's not easy to satisfy—or rather nobody has yet worked out

a satisfactory way of doing it. Here are the main solutions so
far:

- CNN and CBC Newsworld, using conventional news
  format, but in all-news channels. Actually, in the 1940s,
  in the early days of TV, viewers were prepared to watch
  continuous flows of news ticker tape across the screen,
  until the networks came up with the evening news formula
  that's still in use today, half a century later.

- Targeted messages like direct mail and advertising aimed
  at a particular income group, whether for politics or to
  explain issues.

- Talk shows and phone-in interview shows. These shows,
  for example *Larry King Live* and its Newsworld equivalent or CBC Radio's *Cross Country Check Up*, amount to
  town meetings with an electronic extension. These programs allow viewers to speak directly to politicians and
  other public personalities without the use of professional
  questioners (although some hosts will follow up when the
  guest appears to slide away from a point raised by a caller).

  Often, too, callers will follow up each other. American
  cable broadcaster C-Span, which, like Canadian
  RogersCable, broadcasts news events in their entirety
  (Congressional or Parliamentary hearings, speeches and
  so on), also has phone-in segments that have developed
  an active following of people who are actually well-
  informed on issues and who will pin a guest who tries
  evasive tactics—often clobbering the guest with well-
  researched quotes of previous statements he or she has
  made. Because they're viewers interested in information,
  not reporters trying to get a headline, they can be relent-
  less. C-Span's viewer call-in segments, with guests well-
  publicized in advance, can be a treat to watch.

- Computer services, such as Compuserve, Dow Jones,
  Dialog and Nexis—to name just a few—offer gateways
  to full texts of news tickers, magazines, scholarly journals

and dissertation abstracts, torrents of news and information that has to be used to be appreciated. This stuff is an info freak's wet dream. In the hands of a skilled researcher, these services yield an information bounty on any subject.

The last two versions come closest to following the "laws" of the information economy. They push choice downstream to the viewer or searcher. Each person can get what he or she wants out of it. Unlike the first two variations, there is no packaged offering confronting the viewer, deciding for the viewer what he or she ought to be interested in. The conventional news—whether print or electronic—makes all these choices for the viewer: what to be interested in and how much time to devote to it.

The logical consequence of this is that the class of people known as news editors or lineup editors in print and electronic media have lost their purpose. What keeps them hanging around now is that the technology that allows viewers to select the programs or program segments they want is still not that easy to use and is certainly too tough for average people with average levels of interest to use.

One choice most of us would like is to be able to program our televisions to tell us that part of the news we want to hear—not what someone else tells us. This technology is available through the automatic selection features of the newswire services. You can program your computer to select certain types of stories from the news flow and not others.

Some of us may find this disquieting. Most of us long for a friendly, intellectual father figure to tell us what it all means, rather than trying to understand it for ourselves. Says Lloyd Barber, "I used to think that more education of media types would improve the quality of journalism... Having created a school of journalism at the University of Regina, I'm not sure I didn't just turn out the same people with more credentials. Where are the James M. Minifies [Canadian

broadcast journalist]? Where are the Malcolm Muggeridges?
Where are the people who command respect by reason of
the sheer intellectual quality of their contribution?" The
solution is simple: give us a choice of gurus. That's what's
powering the newsletter revolution. That, plus the extraordinary desktop publishing explosion that has revolutionized
the printing business.

It has become something of a cliché but still amazing. This
post-Gutenberg revolution means you can put a print shop and
news operation into place on your kitchen table, all for less than
$5,000. It's impossible to deny that, combined with the market
characteristics we've already mentioned, the information economy is pushing choice down to the individual—a downward-
to-individual empowerment. The market for newsletters is narrow
and deep, instead of broad and shallow. The result is an explosion of specialized information demand—4,500 newsletters today
versus 2,200 ten years ago. The start-up cost: $25,000, mainly for
mailing, promotion and so on. The price differences: $30 to $50
for consumer letters, $200 to $300 for a good business letter.
(Higher price letters target smaller groups.)

Amazingly, another branch of news that may actually survive is that of trade publications. Statistics Canada data shows
Canadian magazines have been accomplishing the near impossible: making revenues grow at a time of plummeting circulation. From 1989 to 1990, the last period for which figures
are available, Canadian magazine circulation nosedived, falling
six percent for the first time in eight years. And this was before
the GST really dampened subscriber enthusiasm. Since then,
according to the Canadian Magazine Publishers Association,
there's been another drop of as much as six percent. Yet at
the same time, Statscan noted that revenues from advertising
inched up one percent. (Again, there are no figures for 1991,
when the recession really began gobbling ad budgets; the
CMPA and Statistics Canada both predict that things have
since become much grimmer.)

Bearing that in mind, what's happening out there? Who are the casualties? How are the survivors keeping their financial heads above water? And who is crazy enough to launch new publications at a time like this?

(To illustrate the news/information point further, what follows is based on a news story—but because we're surrounding it with context and background, it has become information supporting a general line of argument.)

- *Canadian Speeches/Issues*, a small magazine published 10 times a year out of Woodville, Ontario, has just celebrated its fifth birthday. Despite an impressive array of contributors ranging from Margaret Thatcher to Nelson Mandela to Pierre Berton, George Erasmus, Jacques Parizeau and Brian Mulroney, the magazine's editorial costs are zip. Why? Because publisher-editor Earle Gray just collects the Great Ones' speeches (he's on the mailing list of a lot of clubs, service organizations and governments). Gray's main costs are production (paper and offset press printing) and mailing. The small, handbook-sized publication has 1,000 subscribers, many of whom are politicians, students and professional speech writers. It's also available on-line.

- *Herizons*, a Winnipeg-based feminist magazine, has risen from the ashes of the old *Herizons*, a glossy-paper publication that died in 1987. More modest than its predecessor, the mag is designed, rather handsomely, on desktop in a tiny room in the editor's house, is printed on bond rather than glossy paper, and is mostly black-and-white. Subscriptions reached 3,000 the day the first issue came back from the printer's. *Herizons* depends on subscriber, not advertiser, support. But to survive, *Herizons* reckons it has to reach 10,000 readers within the next four years.

- *Tree House* is a new quarterly emphasizing nature-oriented activities for families. It reaches 220,000 Canadian

households stapled into the middle of *Owl* and *Chickadee*,
children's magazines. Unlike the host magazines in which
it's carried, *Tree House* carries ads, lots of ads.

What About Electronic Media?

How do the trends we've been discussing affect the electronic
media, that is, radio and TV? They felt the information pressures earliest, and the effects show up in what's been happening to these media since the mid-1980s. The most
conspicuous trend seems to be the changing position of the networks in North America. The former arbiters of public taste
in the United States, especially CBS, but also NBC and ABC,
have ceased to be controlled by broadcasters and are now
controlled by businesspeople. In Canada, the same trend is
shown most clearly in the decision of the CBC to accept advertising and to restructure.

These changes are related to the increasing problems with the
broadcasters' traditional pricing formula: free TV to deliver
a national audience for which advertisers will pay. Make no
mistake. Broadcasting in the United States is still extremely
profitable, thanks in part to the cost cutting introduced by the
advertising-funded networks' new owners. Nevertheless, each
year shows a slow and steady decline in the audience share
enjoyed by the advertising-funded networks and growth of
cable TV's share. Networks' viewership has slipped from seventy percent in 1983 to fifty-seven percent in 1991. To be sure,
much of the growth of competition may have leveled off. But
cable continues to be more attractive to advertisers.

In the United States, network TV advertising is growing at
about twice the rate of the economy overall, although in some
years, like 1985, it declined. The big three U.S. networks'
gains are also vulnerable to competition by the emerging
fourth network, Rupert Murdoch's Fox Movie Channel. U.S.
cable companies, although much smaller, are still riding a

growth wave. Revenue is growing at more than twenty percent a year, and even network analysts admit cable advertising revenues are outpacing those of the networks. On the other hand, all segments, cable and network, are facing significant cost pressure from their program suppliers. This is putting pressure on pricing formulae.

In Canada, there are some twelve communication companies with a total of $4 billion in assets. Three of those companies—the CBC, Baton and Global—control more than half the assets. Broadcast and cable companies alike are underperforming the stock market averages at the moment. These numbers show what we all know already, namely that cable has moved from being an ally of broadcasting to being its most immediate competitor. As well, they suggest a competitive weakness among the smaller players in the industry in Canada.

What accounts for this? Analysts put the industry outlook down to the relatively high degree of competition and regulatory uncertainty. Another factor, too, is the CBC. The CBC's status enables it to run a deficit even when the rest of the industry makes money. Whether for good or ill, this constitutes a sizable distortion in a market, with built-in instability because of the nature of its information product and the way we've chosen to regulate it. For example, policies like Canadian content mean the CBC produces too much of what no one watches and not enough of what might be sold globally.

Currently, we're witnessing a "war for the wire" between cable companies and telecommunications companies (telcos) like Bell and Unitel being fought out in the regulatory arena. Communications are regulated in Canada by the Canadian Radio/Television Commission (CRTC). It regulates broadcast, cable and telephone as though they were different industries, as indeed they were a couple of decades ago. But they aren't now. The new technology, especially fiber-optic cable, transmits pictures, voices and data with equal ease. Technology

and market forces are challenging the regulatory framework
to get out of the way lest it cripple Canada's global lead in
this area.

The separation among cable, free network TV and telecommunications services is being dissolved by the same forces
of technological change and entrepreneurial instinct as occurred
in financial services in the 1980s. Until the mid-1980s, there
were few problems with the way we partitioned broadcast,
cable and telephone communication. That comfort disappeared after 1985. In Canada, seventy percent of homes have
access to cable and more than half have VCRs. The VCR,
with its ad-zapping capability, decimates broadcast TV, that
is, "free" TV paid for by advertisers. Cable, equally vulnerable to ad zapping, nevertheless gives viewers more choice.
If the phone companies have their way, they'll offer everything
over a single wire into a home entertainment center. When
that happens, it promises a new generation of interactive TV
viewing, including delayed viewing (TV on demand) and
more viewer choice that effectively makes the viewer the program editor. (Indeed, this technology is now available to cable
subscribers in Montreal.)

In addition, in Canada and Europe, there's rising pressure
from satellite broadcasters for greater access to national systems. The point here is that the technology is so simple, that
people all over Europe—even in eastern Europe—have rigged
up makeshift dishes to snatch CNN. You can hear them on
the morning call-in programs, interviewing U.S. journalists
and members of Congress. Satellite services in North America
also carry with them the possibility of bypassing phone networks and using so-called "smart building" technology to
find the cheapest route available for information transmission. Satellite technology allows video carriers to put pressure on the phone companies, instead of vice versa, but—and
it's a big but—only where regulation encourages cross subsidizing of local services by long-distance.

There's also competition between networks and local broadcasting. This competition has resulted in a search for new ways to mass market network TV, apart from the news, and in the increasingly popular formula of using company tie-ins to attract viewers to follow network seasonal programming. NBC has a tie-in with McDonald's; K-Mart joins in promoting CBS's lineup. These promotions are akin to car makers' rebates to lure viewers lost to cable's vertical programming or local stations, including an embryo "fourth network," Fox TV. The independents can have closer tie-ins with production companies, such as Sony's Columbia. This has re-opened the debate about syndication, that is, the right to acquire program distribution rights.

However significant these developments may be, there's a broader strategic problem facing the networks. In the United States, broadcasters, despite declining market shares, remain extremely profitable. But they're facing rising production costs and increasing competition from cable, which is gradually becoming more profitable as it pays down the costs of wiring eighty-five percent of the U.S. domestic market. What's more, the main constraint on growth of traditional broadcasting is the fact that most of the advertisers are made up of relatively mature industries with established brand names. These companies are operating primarily in a defensive mode and are unwilling to raise prices to pay for more advertising. Instead, they're putting the heat on agency commissions.

This is a far cry from the 1950s, when the growth of television was financed by the post-war expansion of corporate America—the same industries that are now mature and reluctant or unable to spend more on advertising. In addition, the information economy has killed advertising as an instrument of mass consumption. The VCR and the remote control allow viewers to zap commercials. So the audience that prompted the companies to spend big bucks targeting commercials can no longer be guaranteed by the broadcasters.

On the other hand, the same company sponsors are increasingly willing to spend on improved telecommunications—such as direct phone communication with customers and potential customers. (Nissan, for example, includes a toll-free number to all vehicle purchasers. North American car manufacturers are following.) Indeed, telecommunications profit growth has been the fastest of all U.S. corporate segments in 1992. Narrow and deep is better than broad and shallow. In Canada, a similar grim logic applies. Total ad revenues of $1.3 billion supply a little over half the operating revenues of the industry (CBC included). Much of the local advertising that might be expected to shift from print to TV is retail. The retail sector is particularly GNP-sensitive, and the 1990s has so far been a slow-growth decade. The telecommunications segment has a much healthier growth outlook than traditional broadcasting, especially in an economy powered mainly by business capital investment.

The North American Outlook for Broadcast News

In the short run, broadcasting in the United States will continue to outperform cable and will provide to production companies and advertisers alike the most direct routes to a mass audience. This preference reflects a particular way of doing business, and as long as companies wish to market their products in this way, the service is unlikely to disappear.

For Canadians, that means good returns for the suppliers of U.S. programming to Canadian viewers. It also means good years for Canadian producers of shows and superior services destined for the U.S. market. The trouble with this scenario is the Canadian content rules. Exports of Canadian shows to U.S. cable networks may offer a way to work around this constraint. For example, high-end Canadian content such as *Anne of Green Gables* can be sold worldwide and counted as an export. Since it also counts as Canadian content, the more we sell abroad, the more schlock we can show at home. A real problem in Canada is the competitive weakness of the players. A shakeout is inevitable—we may already be seeing it in Montreal—especially as the CBC moves to a more commercial footing.

In the longer run the battle will likely go to the big battalions of the telecommunications service companies. The big networks and the big studios are about the same size—between $1 billion and $5 billion in sales. The big telecommunications operations are between $3 billion and $13 billion. It would cost just over $100 billion to buy all the cable and broadcast TV stations in the United States. That amount is about equal to the annual revenue stream of the major telecommunications service companies in the United States, and one-fifth the total revenue stream of the big equipment suppliers. In Canada, the total operating revenue of broadcast and cable is barely equal to Bell Canada's long distance revenues (about $3 billion). If the telcos win, Canadian broadcast and cable will cease to exist in their present form.

A Look at the Future

Almost everybody in North America talks on the telephone and watches TV. Today the two systems are being drawn together by technology.

The technologists say compatibility of cable, phone and computer in Canada will be completed within five years. The whole country will be home and office-wired with fiber optic cable within ten years. The bill for this is not inconsiderable. It's turning out to be higher than we may wish to pay. But since most of the services envisaged for fiber can already be provided over existing infrastructure, it looks as if the pace of change depends on the regulatory environment. If the government allows telecommunications companies, TV stations and cable networks to combine in single entities, Canadian broadcasting as we know it might end in two years—and that might make fiber-optic cabling more affordable.

What practical conclusions, if any, flow from these considerations? If the foregoing is at all accurate, how information is distributed will be an area of some instability for the next few years. When that is sorted out, there'll be an explosion in the demand for new programs (because of fiber-optic and enhanced-coaxial cable). These will have to compete with other services, perhaps aimed at home computers. Producing content, then, is the key to the future—the same future that ABC's production company, Capital Cities and Disney, to name but two big players, have already started deploying their forces to meet. In Canada, we may have to recognize that in one respect at least Marshall McLuhan was wrong—content does matter. Big shows, with big production values, win big audiences world wide.

Second, given the scale of things in Canada, forget the idea that our "cultural" industries are protected. We need to think of markets in global terms and go for exports in order to make high quality affordable.

Third, we should take advantage of domestic competition to hone our products for export. Take news. Instead of producing ethnic news only for Canadians, we should consider syndicating it to ethnic home markets; instead of producing business news for Canadian investors we should make it suitable for syndication to major capital centres, and so on. We already have some good examples of shows produced for highly focused Canadian audiences that can be profitably syndicated to similar audiences in other countries. We should build on those kinds of programs.

Fourth, we should make the Canadian content rules work for us—Canadian high culture has international resonance, if the New York bestseller lists can be believed. World-class productions of top Canadian material for showing throughout the English-speaking world would generate and hold a huge audience. The United States has virtually abdicated high quality TV drama, leaving it to Commonwealth countries. Well, let's exploit that.

Fifth, the risks of foreign distribution can be significantly reduced with coproductions and joint ventures. We may have missed the boat with respect to cable start-ups in the United States, but there are new boats leaving every day, and we should get aboard some of them.

Sixth, let's explore the creation of programs or services that make full use of emerging interactive technologies. There may be some products that would gain value from exclusivity—for example, high-level executive briefings with leading specialists in different subjects. These could be distributed electronically. Spin-offs of some of the interviews could be sold as special videotapes and not aired at all. Education services may work in this regard, too—for example, a series of professional development seminars targeted at the needs of specific groups could be distributed via national associations in some way.

As for the ten o'clock news? (Or the nine o'clock news?) Like the *Globe and Mail*, and other media that attempt to be something for everybody, the nightly news formula has lost its audience and is now mainly an expensive bulletin board for the powerful and the policy nerds. Most people don't want news, they want information and they want it the way they want it—cut to their tastes, not the editors'. Now technology can cater to this demand. Only the regulations stand in the way.

Nine

The Business of Education: Try Advertising

*Smartness runs in my family. When I went to
school, I was so smart my teacher was in my
class for five years.*

—George Burns

*Children enter school as question marks and
leave as periods.*

—Neil Postman

COULD IT BE that our education system is actually broken
beyond repair? Consider: today, advanced societies spend billions trying to pass on ideas, concepts and knowledge—but
we're still doing it inadequately.

Canada spends a whopping $43 billion a year on education
at all levels. That's a lot of money. Our total construction budget, residential and commercial, is in the same ball park—
$58 billion a year. We buy around $36 billion worth of new
cars and spend about $39 billion in food stores. We spend
about half as much in department stores and service stations
as we do on education. The point of the comparisons is that

118

the education dollar amount is what you might expect for a large sector of the economy. What's disappointing is not the money but the results. Here's what the (now defunct) Economic Council of Canada recently reported:

- We spend more on education than most countries.
- The system turns out a population in which more than one in four Canadians aged sixteen to twenty-four is functionally illiterate and forty-four percent are functionally innumerate.
- The current dropout rate before secondary school leaving is around thirty percent (almost the same as the illiteracy rate).
- A strikingly high proportion of those who can read and follow simple instructions lack the problem-solving skills needed to give us the competitive edge in the international workplace.
- The full-time enrolment rate in engineering and applied science has been dropping steadily since 1983. Fewer than twenty-five percent of high school graduates take advanced courses in science and math.
- Even fewer high school students—less than ten percent— take vocational skills training courses, although less than forty percent of high school entrants actually go on to university. There is thus a large population of unqualified people entering the work force after high school.

Not, of course, that there aren't more cases of success than failure—after all, *only* thirty percent of our high school kids drop out, and *only* twenty-five percent of our work force is illiterate (can't read a bus schedule), and *only* forty-four percent is functionally innumerate (can't add up a restaurant check). That means that for seventy percent of our high school students and between fifty-six and seventy-five percent of our work force, the system has been more or less adequate. Remember when Pierre Trudeau couldn't understand why we were upset at a ten percent unemployment rate? After all, he told his audience, ninety percent of people who wanted to work were working. Trudeau's answer didn't cut it then, and the success rate of our education system doesn't cut it now. Even though it ain't broke, we can't say it ain't in desperate need of repair. The fact is that we, as citizens and taxpayers, parents and employers, have taken our eyes off this particular ball, and it's now bouncing around without direction, out of control.

Says Hugh McDiarmid, cofounder and president of Stormont Investments, owners of the Ottawa Senators: "The priority is to rekindle the willingness of Canadians to invest in our country. And it's not just business. It's education. Education is the single most important long-term investment that we make, yet our universities are starving and our public school systems are increasingly under funding pressure."

"We Know Better Than You"

Most of the solutions proposed suggest more centralized controls from government or from special stakeholder groups such as business and labor to improve skills training, strengthen the school-to-work transition and encourage the production of more maths and sciences graduates. But how well will this mesh with what we've already discovered about the information-based global economy?

The analysis of and solutions for how we educate our children are too much tinted with an industrial-society perspective. An information-age view starts with the recognition that our contemporary education system, like much of the "software" of the industrial age, was designed for an industrial purpose. With the encroachment of industrial organization on an essentially agricultural society around 1900 came the creation of highly structured institutions—hospitals for birth, death and healing, courthouses for lawyering, cities for manufacturing, schools for education, all time-, place- and manner-bound, each performed within the confines of the appropriate hallowed halls under the official auspices of the right specialist. But what's the point of going to school if your home computer can access several libraries full of information and link you with like-minded people around the world who want to discuss what you want to discuss? Why pay money to hear the local prof when the world's leading expert is available on a videocassette or on a satellite channel?

We give lip service to the idea that knowledge, information and learning are the economy's primary resources and that education needs to become a lifelong process of learning. We all know that we can't get anywhere without an education (we need junior matriculation to become an apprentice gas pumper, high school leaving papers to train as a mechanic), but we fail to give sufficient weight to the transience of what we learn. We live in a world in which research not only adds to our knowledge, but removes it, as well. The value of what we learn today is increasingly fragile: recent estimates suggest that knowledge in the fastest growing natural and social sciences has a half-life of perhaps five years; that is, half of what we learn today will be shown to be wrong or irrelevant within five years. Says futurist John Kettle, "Assuming two graduates started out in 1986 with a headful of knowledge, one in an enduring discipline such as structural engineering or family medicine, the other in something that is developing explosively (biogenetics or electronics, say), the engineer would reach retirement with almost a fifth of his college learning still valid, while the biogeneticist would be down to that level only fifteen years after graduation—in her mid-thirties, probably."

Taking Ownership

The information revolution is about individual empowerment and about flat, decentralized organizations instead of vertical, centralized ones. Any education system designed for the global information economy has to be able to contribute to it. And the premiere requirement for the 1990s is to give ourselves a whack on the head every so often to encourage creativity and innovative solutions. Canada's education costs are among the industrial world's highest, but the output, at least as measured in international test scores, is among the industrial world's worst. That's because we have a misallocation of resources: we're trying to work against markets instead of with them.

One basic problem is that all schools cost the same. The education debate at the moment is calling for smarter schools and different ways of organizing what is still essentially a socialized sector. That is, for the most part, the education system is a public service, paid for with taxpayer money. But experience suggests that socialism never works. Even Nancy Riche, vice president of the Canadian Labor Congress, says, "The decision on training hasn't been made in context. Training is just one word, and workers are saying 'training doesn't mean you have a job. Training doesn't mean full employment. Training is not a job.' "

As things stand today, students crowd to good schools where there's a choice. And when there's no choice, well, parents have to take what they get. If we're going to solve the problem, we need another perspective on it. Only the combination of competition and prices that reflect perceptions of value effectively delivers the goods. That's true whether we're talking about cars or VCRs or accounting services—or education. The easiest way to reallocate resources on a rational basis is to give all students an equal "fund" of education credits and let them spend them as they or their parents see fit. The education credits, sometimes called the voucher system, would be valid in any learning facility, public or private. So anyone in receipt of the credits will be off to the school of choice. Should the best schools have entrance exams to screen the horde of applicants? Well, right away, you can see how injecting choice into the system will bring back standards. And right away you can see the likelihood of an explosion of commercial establishments supplying consumer education demands. (Even now, the private sector, including employers, spends more on training than the public does.)

There's a great deal of resistance to these proposals among the educational establishment in schools, and above all in provincial education ministries. The only rational explanation of the resistance is vested interest: they'd rather substitute their judgment for that of the clients of the system. It's as though General Motors could order you to drive a Pontiac or Chevrolet because there was a dealer in your neighborhood—instead of letting you buy the Toyota or Honda you want. If we won't tolerate that system for cars, why do we tolerate it for something as important as education? North American students spend more time with TV and video games than they do at school. They have more technology at home and at work than they do in the schools. And schools are tremendously bureaucratic places, filled with an aging work force whose salaries are linked to the number of years of service instead of to results. In meeting our education objectives, we can't be sentimental or nostalgic. We have to put together a knowledge-based industry to create the citizens and the labor force of tomorrow, today.

We argue constantly about education in Canada being a provincial responsibility, but that's a myth in the information age, and a costly one, at that. There's nothing to prevent you or your kids (or anyone else) from taking your education by correspondence from other provinces, states or countries, even now. And with computers and telecommunications, interactive TV and so on, we can all learn what we want to learn when and where we want to learn it. An awful lot of us haven't yet turned on to the fact that we can go to twelve universities by computer, that our children can participate in science projects with children from other countries, that, in fact, the provinces have already lost control of this process. We're still operating our "installed base" (this is the way we've always done it) by inertia. But we don't have to. It could change tomorrow.

Education is a $40 billion-plus business in Canada and is struggling to adjust itself to the new environment. But it's a tough fight, because not enough top people have figured out how to think about things yet. At the Open Learning Agency in British Columbia, Glenn Farrell and Lucille Pacey, president and vice president respectively, are convinced that "You can create a new world out there just with some policy changes about what you're going to treat as a legitimate activity." Here's what they're talking about.

Most ministries of education and advanced education understand the need to build buildings. So there are capital budgets set aside for the bricks and mortar. Telecommunications networks aren't considered capital investments as are buildings. If they were, access to learning would increase significantly overnight. That's the kind of restructuring in the thinking process we need.

Other thinking processes in other heads also need restructuring. Federal communications regulators need to reconsider rates structures, so that network users can provide services on demand, pay for what they use and not be forced to pay for a pipeline they don't use all the time.

Right now, there's a huge potential manufacturing sector in Canada that's hobbled in its development by totally inappropriate structures. Getting rid of those structures—or at least melting them down to manageable dimensions—will be critical to making this area succeed. For example, the people who run traditional educational organizations seem to believe that going to school in person is the only legitimate way to learn. So even if they have extension departments or continuing education units, or in some cases dedicated distance education units, these have been starved of funds and forced to operate at the margin. ("We're not going to put real base dollars into this kind of thing...") Glenn Farrell says, "These departments have been pretty much restricted and forced to operate as a mafia. Even though they've formed networks and associations across the country, they themselves are the first to tell people from other provinces: stay out of my turf. ... Because they've been forced to earn their own money to survive, they don't want competition coming from outside the province."

But what's rapidly making that way of thinking obsolete is the use of telecommunication technology and networks. And as that increases over the next decade, boundaries will mean less and less. As things now stand, this very powerful manufacturing sector is locked into the essentially socialist structure of a provincial university. And, like all Eastern European economies, it's trying to break free and become a revenue generator. And like several other institutions in Canada (such as the International Business Centre at Montreal's Ecole des Hautes Etudes commerciales), it is succeeding in the marketplace—mainly by adopting the open, alliance-based structures that characterize knowledge-based industries in general. The Open Learning Agency generates almost a third of its operating revenue, substantially more than other publicly funded educational institutions. It's committed to raising more, by marketing its instructional materials all over the world and by acting as marketing agent for materials produced by other institutions. Farrell says, "We're very committed to the idea of partnerships. The kind of vision that we have for this place will never ever be realized if we were just to rely on government funding. What we do is look for strategic alliances, partnerships of one kind or another." OLA has a partnership with BC Hydro. BC Hydro underwrites programs it is interested in, say, related to the environment and energy conservation. BC Hydro gets recognition and the network gets to run some of the specific stuff.

The partnership idea is paying off, especially with larger, global corporations, such as Xerox, the office equipment megafirm whose research pioneered the user-friendly designs brought to consumer markets by Apple computers and now matched worldwide. Farrell: "Xerox is in the printing business. We're one of the largest educational publishers in the country—nearly thirty million pages a year. So they developed some new technology that enables us to move toward printing on demand. We're the first in the country to have fully linked an electronic publishing platform with their publishing-on-demand printing capability. From Xerox's point of view, we're a showplace. We have an agreement with them: when they start selling this equipment to other customers, if that customer needs staff trained, they may look to us to provide the training."

Xerox is one of the foremost companies in North America in terms of their commitment to quality management. One way of putting quality management into education is to look further afield than the educational establishment for solutions. Here's an example: there's good reason to believe that advertising is among those industries being transformed beyond recognition by the changes taking place in the world. And before you remember George Orwell's line about advertising ("the stick rattling in the swill bucket"), think again about the perfection of both the timing and the fit with education. But to link the future of advertising in a knowledge economy to its potential future in education requires a short sidebar.

The Images of Affluence

Start by asking yourself: where did the global marketplace come from? Scratch any economist and he or she is apt to say something like, "It's the product of two generations of postwar trade and investment, mainly by multinational companies. The result has brought approximately equal living standards in the developed world along with homogenization of tastes and consumer buying habits." They might add something about technology shrinking space and time through jet travel and telecommunications.

But what's the reality behind this arcane formula? Just this: more and more people in more and more countries wanted to buy and were able to buy the same products from the same manufacturers. In fact, they wanted to do it so much that they pulled down trade barriers, nontariff barriers, hosted foreign investment and so on. And what drove those desires was, as much as anything, the images of affluence created by advertising.

Being rich in medieval times meant being a king with castles and a standing army. Before World War I, it meant being a member of a select group of boring if lavishly attired men and women going to the opera. Now, even in the frugal nineties, rich means sun and sensuality, preferably Mediterranean or Californian; rich means sunglasses and sexy clothing with an Italian look. It means cars by Mercedes, shoes by Gucci, pens by Cross, credit cards colored gold; it means Hermès, Concorde... Luxuries, yes, but luxuries that are also accessible, not only to the rich but the moderately well-off.

Despite all the ups of the mid eighties and the downs of the late eighties and early nineties, the top ten brands in the world (Coca-Cola, Pepsi-Cola, Rolex, Gucci, Cardin, Sony, Mercedes Benz, Levi Strauss, Cross and Hermès) have remained as stable as a rock. This is the power of advertising. If you think of the world as being the pictures in our heads, most of those pictures have been created by advertising. The global marketplace is the marketplace dominated by the fabulously successful marketing campaigns of Mercedes-Benz, Pepsi, Levi's, Rolex, Gucci, Cardin, Sony. Before it's anything else, the concept of globalization is a marketer's slogan, supported by a brilliant portfolio of global product icons.

Now, globalization has rendered the traditional advertising agency out of date. The mass market has shriveled. Brand loyalties are disintegrating. Consumers are becoming choosier, wanting price and quality comparisons before they buy. And there's the question of whether we can handle any more advertising. With some three thousand messages a day hitting our heads, even winning a fraction of a second's attention is a nearly impossible challenge. Clearly, the ad industry is in for a rough ride. The relative financial weakness of the industry together with its limited scope will render it less than attractive to the most creative brains we have. Unless...

The Great Transformation

What's coming is a long shot, something we don't have yet. In this view, there will still be agencies that employ creative people as communicators. They'll have mastery of the emerging multimedia technologies, including cyberspace or virtual reality. And their role will be something like special-effects people, of Disney-type "imagineering" specialists. These people will be organized into firms more like today's advertising shops than anything else. But they will be educators, not advertisers. And they will essentially take over society's teaching role.

Kids are interested in all sorts of things and have the staying power to do well in those subjects if they get some encouragement. But schools that reduce self-esteem and make things seem more difficult than necessary may not be the best learning environments for everyone. And today and in the future everyone has to learn. So one way or another, whether based on libraries as community information centers, or arcades with education games that are more fun than Mario Brothers, we will educate ourselves and our children. Or rather, we and the children will do it ourselves, based on individual buying decisions.

It is to this endeavor that the bulk of today's advertising skills could be applied: from creating the bridges to knowledge, to tracking learning progress, to plotting media strategies for special educational products. Advertisers won't actually produce the knowledge, any more than they build the cars they sell. Mercedes-Benz engineers may build great cars. But they still need advertising to sell them. Similarily, even though advertisers don't make physics or reading skills they can help children absorb them. The market they will "sell" to will be parents and children, and people of all ages in a continuous learning culture.

That brings us to cost. What looks like a lot of money as a collective decision—namely education budgets—is a rather respectable amount seen as a sum total of consumer decisions. For example, a $40 billion sector in a $700 billion economy is significant if it grows out of consumer choice. And winning market share for one consumer product or another is what advertisers do best.

So suppose we had a couple of national testing periods— maybe involving a couple of weeks away from home two or three times in your life—along with, say, semiannual local or provincial tests at other times. And then we left the choice of how best to meet those testing requirements to parents and children—albeit with a reasonable amount of consumer protection.

That's akin to the way we run the housing market. Or the car market. And we get better houses and we get better cars than we get education for our students. One big challenge of the nineties is how to take a basket-case $43 billion dollar Canadian education industry and make it a world leader. Canadian advertisers may well have the skills to bring the educational experience of the best to the rest by using new technologies and the wonderful creativity of which the industry has always been capable.

Ten

The Business of the Social Safety Net

*"I'm not returning until you fix it," Count
Basie told a nightclub owner whose piano
was always out of tune. A month later Basie
was called that everything was okay. When
he returned, the piano was still out of tune.
"You said you fixed it!" an irate Basie
exclaimed. "I did," came the reply. "I had it
painted."*

—*quoted Roger von Oech in*
A Whack On the Side of the Head

TAP A HUNDRED Canadians at random, and the likelihood is that
ninety-nine of them will cite our social safety net as the program
that most distinguishes our society from that of our closest
neighbors, biggest trading partners and toughest competitors.

But our social programs take big bucks to deliver. And in
a global economy, the particular programs that seem to have
served us well in the industrial economy, and of which
Canadians are proud and fond, are now making the adjustment process slower and more difficult. They may even be
preventing it.

This chapter is here so we can examine our social safety net, look at the bill and suggest some ways public concerns might be handled in an open, global, information-based economy. We can get the problems of the safety net under control and mend all the holes in it by operating in a clearheaded manner, respecting a little basic economics and taking full advantage of new financial technologies. For in some ways the funding problem for social programs should be easier in the new economy if we can be flexible enough to approach the problem a little differently.

Middle income people are the major beneficiaries of public services such as education (public school from kindergarten to grade twelve is free, and university courses are priced below market value) and universally accessible medical care. Middle income earners are also the people most at risk from the economic changes arising from global competition (among the jobs lost are what used to be known as "good" jobs: salaried middle managers with lots of company benefits). So it makes good economic sense, if you're one of these people, to want as much of these public services as you can get.

Remember the inflationary 1970s, when a lot of people thought they were getting better off because their salaries were rising every year? That was an "income illusion," because prices were rising just as fast. A great many "average" Canadians are, in the 1990s, chasing a "security illusion." They believe that our prosperity and our social safety net will be at risk if we try to get into the competitive fray. Trouble is, the analysis is not just faulty, it's flagrantly wrong. The more we fight adapting to the market, the more vulnerable our prosperity and social programs become. Because unless we open our markets, we won't be able to access other markets, and there's only a certain number of goods we can make and sell to each other. The misinformed campaigns of emotional Luddites such as Mel Hurtig and Maude Barlow, if brought to fruition, would take a moderately competitive economy and fossilize it.

Let's be clear about exactly what our social safety net is. A comprehensive list would include:

- Unemployment insurance
- Medicare, including provincial programs and federal transfers
- Canada Assistance Plan and provincial social assistance
- Old age security, the Guaranteed Income Supplement
- Canada Pension Plan/Quebec Pension Plan
- Family Allowances, child tax credits, child-care deductions
- Equalization payments
- Social housing programs.

You could also include education because it's a substantial part of our public sector overhead. But there's an argument for excluding it if you strictly define social programs as income maintenance.

- Primary and secondary education
- Post-secondary education, including provincial programs and federal transfers
- Training programs.

Although they're not, strictly speaking, income maintenance programs, you could argue that regional development programs should be included because they're part of our social overhead.

Some of the expenses, like unemployment insurance, are directly linked to the performance of the economy as a whole. They go up when the economy goes down. The outlays are therefore always changing, both absolutely and as a function of GNP, making them difficult to predict. Nor are they constant across the country. Given Canada's great regional differences, the economy operates differently in different areas. In 1992 central Canada was in something like free fall, while Alberta and British Columbia were still experiencing positive growth. This disparity also affects the flow (and amount) of equalization payments.

There are some exceptions. Old Age Security is not tied to the economy. It is a function of demographics. Since people are living longer and the baby-boomer bulge is moving through our population profile, this amount is unlikely to diminish anytime soon.

Another feature of our social safety net is the way it's affected by our complicated constitutional arrangements. Health, education and social welfare are provincial responsibilities under the BNA Act. But the vague wording of these sections has allowed Ottawa to use its so-called spending power to ensure comparable social service standards nationwide. What's more, fiscal transfers include cash and so-called tax points, that is, the right to occupy certain amounts of particular tax fields. And as Ottawa increasingly acts like a cash-strapped government, the proportion of cash it's transferring to the provinces is falling relative to the proportion of tax transfers.

A corollary of these arrangements, as many observers have long remarked, is a striking absence of coordination between provincial and federal levels. When one lowers taxes, the other is likely to raise them. The same thing happens on the spending side, as the 1992 Ontario budget showed. When Ottawa makes an effort at spending restraint, the provinces have the power to rush in with new spending. As tax transfers grow relative to cash transfers, this lack of coordination is likely to increase.

In evaluating the burden of these programs, the most meaningful figure is the share of GDP or GNP we devote to these things. Just to show you the pattern: on a consolidated basis, total Canadian government spending has grown from thirty-one percent of GDP in the mid-1960s to forty-six percent today. Since provincial spending has grown from about twelve percent of GDP to about twenty-three percent today, the feds and the provinces spend about the same amount of tax dollars.

The same is true on the revenue side. On a consolidated basis, the total government take has grown from twenty-seven percent of GDP in 1965 to around forty percent today. And the increase is almost entirely attributable to the provinces.

If you look solely at programs—that is, if you take debt service out as well as transfers—the pattern remains the same, although the percentages become more tolerable. In 1968, federal program spending amounted to about twelve percent of GDP. Provincial and local came to eight percent each. Total program spending thus came to about twenty-eight percent of GDP.

Today local spending is actually a little less, around seven percent of GDP. Federal program spending is now about twelve and a half percent. And the provinces? They've grown to be about the same as Ottawa. So total program spending in Canada, net of transfers and debt service, amounts to about thirty-one percent of GDP.

Is This Big Business or What?

It's hard to appreciate the scale these proportions represent, unless you compare them with something else. At thirty-one percent of GDP, our social program spending effort is larger than our whole trading sector, which represents about twenty-five percent of GNP. The amount spent on programs at all levels of governments dwarfs the amount we trade with the United States, which is just under twenty percent of GNP. Now let's look at the dollar costs of these programs. We spend about $43 billion on education, around eight percent of GDP; we spend about $48 billion on medical care, around nine percent of GDP.

The Canada Assistance Plan costs about $10 billion (half from Ottawa, half from the provinces); the payout on family allowances is about $2.6 billion annually (a federal program). The Canada Pension Plan pays out about $9.5 billion a year. The Quebec Plan pays out about $2.7 billion a year. The Old Age Security, Guaranteed Income Supplement and Spouse's

Allowance amounts together to about $16 billion. These amounts compare with the country's annual clothing bill, which comes to a bit over $13 billion. Or twice the amount we spend on furniture and appliances, about $7.5 billion.

Beyond looking at the size of the bill, an economist is perhaps equally concerned with what the cost means. Would we be better off if we'd done something else with the money?

Take unemployment insurance. This program should be used to promote transitions to new work. Instead we use it to park people until their old work returns. No wonder we're seeing the marginalization of the work force. Take social assistance, which is what you go on when your pogey runs out. This is organized on the assumption that society owes the worker a job, not vice versa. That is, our programs encourage people to stay put instead of move to where the work is. Peter Gzowski recently asked whether that was more costly than the alternative, which is to encourage people to move to where the work is rather than staying put.

With the greatest respect for Mr. Morningside, the effect of discouraging people from moving is the reverse of what he thinks it is. Instead of giving the region a better chance to recover, we actually worsen its chances. It sounds paradoxical, and it is. You have to understand the economy and the job creation process in dynamic terms. Investment creates jobs. Investment occurs because the market offers a premium return on resources that are not used in consumption.

If jobs are lost, say, in Atlantic Canada, it's because the rewards aren't there for the risk involved, relative to other investment opportunities. For jobs to return, there must be some additional premium paid to capital. What happens if you discourage the movement of labor from, say, Newfoundland? That simply raises the risk—by raising costs— in other parts of Canada. Instead of encouraging investment, it discourages it nationwide. Subsidizing people to wait for jobs is a tide that sinks all boats. As for subsidizing investment? This is a beggar-thy-neighbor game in which everyone loses— including the subsidized investor, unless he or she has taken an additional premium for the political risk associated with the investment.

So how do we measure the cost of programs like those? The main burden is in terms of the market distortions they create. Those problems could be avoided if the programs encouraged market responsiveness instead of impeding it.

Then there's the moral hazard. Moral hazard is what you get when your policies encourage the events they protect against. When savings and loan presidents "misinvest" depositors' money because it's protected by deposit insurance or when life insurance encourages murder, that's moral hazard.

Well, as we all know, the UI we've got encourages work up to the qualification period, after which it encourages unemployment. In the rural areas of the country, UI has become the basis of an informal job sharing program. The practice is sensible from the standpoint of the recipients. They're not encouraged to seek skill upgrading. Nor perhaps would skill upgrading work unless the programs were very carefully designed (do we know enough as trainers to bring it off successfully?). But the fact remains: the programs do encourage unemployment. In general, similar points can be made about all our public programs. Tax-paid "free" public services encourage overconsumption of services.

Anyway, do these programs constitute an opportunity cost? In principle, the answer is "not necessarily." For in a world in which unemployment and poverty are risks, some form of protection is in order. Otherwise, those bearing the risks will seek to survive by other means, including crime. It was only from the 1870s onward that average working people's wages covered their actual expenses. Before that theft, vagabondage and criminal gangs were a normal part of life—as they are again in the United States, albeit for different reasons.

But the important point is that these programs are as big as if not bigger than some of the largest private business sectors in the land. Next question: are they affordable? Well, this is actually a very important question.

Canada's Social Net Is Not an Icon

Before we try to answer this question, this is a good time to point out that there's an incredible amount of humbug being injected into the debate about Canada's social programs. If you listened to the left, you'd think this country has always been in the vanguard of collectivist caring. In the rhetoric of the anti-Free Trade Agreement groups such as organized labor and the Council of Canadians, these programs are achievements, not burdens, that testify to our exceptional national humaneness. In fact, Canada came rather late to the social democratic fold. Europe had well-developed systems of income maintenance, including health care, twenty years before Canada. Canada's depression-driven unemployment insurance and social security programs became law three years after those of the United States. Indeed, Wisconsin had an unemployment insurance scheme in place after World War I. There was nothing like it at the time in Canada.

Franklin Roosevelt, the American president, used the phrase "cradle to grave" to describe desirable social insurance in 1932. It was a long time before any Canadian official used it. Another American New Dealer, Harry Hopkins, pressed for the New Deal Social Security package to include medical care, as well. He was beaten by the American Medical Association, the doctors' lobby. That was in 1935. But the idea wasn't raised in Canada until England's Beveridge Plan (1944) promised a national health service to English men and women. And of course not achieved here until the 1960s.

Still, some people would have us believe that it is our health care system, now a national icon along with the CBC and the

Mounties, that really distinguishes us from the United States. When what actually happened is that the United States has had to choose between a health care system and a defense system for the past fifty years. We, on the other hand, haven't needed a defense budget of any size for thirty years.

This background is worth dwelling on because its acceptance has enabled a government program to be raised to the level of a national icon. That's a major mistake. And it's a strategy that destroys rational discourse, especially about matters of vital public interest. We've got to get this stuff right or we're not going to have it—or very much else.

Despite the rhetoric that's in such plentiful supply, it's amazing how little analysis there is on this simple point: can we afford it all? How should we go about getting a good answer to this question? The question of affordability can be made a lot more precise: does the money spent on these programs generate an equal or greater economic benefit? After all, you could also ask, how do we afford the construction business or the clothing business—economic activities of similar scale. We "afford" them because we pay for them, one house and one coat at a time.

There's a mechanism, called the market, that adjusts price to demand to balance supply and demand. But the mechanism doesn't really exist for social programs. So instead, administration and regulation—the visible hands—take over. But the administrators don't see these programs as businesses. They see them as "macroeconomic policy instruments": stabilizers designed in the 1960s to ward off the depressions of the 1930s.

Take the income maintenance programs, such as social assistance. The argument for social assistance payments is that they act as a stabilizer, preserving purchasing power in a recession. This keeps businesses alive—or at least lessens the shock of a downturn. Social assistance and age-related income programs pump around $26 billion into the economy. In our

$700 billion economy, that's about four percent. No doubt getting a government check, whether people are in or out of work, is an enormous relief. Is it a stabilizer? Very questionable. The first time, yes. But the programs continue. They have now become permanent features of our economy—in good times as well as bad. Social welfare is now an "entitlement." As "entitlements" instead of temporary relief, these programs have a permanent macroeconomic effect. They shift our demand curve upward. They add to demand. And if we add to demand without adding to our production capacity, what do we get? A general rise in prices. Inflation.

That's right. The so-called income maintenance programs—when organized as permanent entitlements—become job killers, not job creators. They just shift resources from production to consumption. They have the same effect as a tax on production. In effect, generous social assistance, once it becomes an entitlement instead of temporary relief, puts a floor under wages. It discourages the creation of certain types of jobs. Where do people go who wanted to work but found the jobs didn't exist? They go on social assistance. Once these income maintainance programs become entitlements, they in effect kill jobs and generate their own clientele. Where should people go if they can't find work? Well, if people capable of earning ten dollars an hour can't find work because welfare generates more than that, they are forced to consider going where welfare doesn't distort the market—Brazil, Chile and Mexico.

Aside from these malevolent effects of income maintainance programs—killing job creation and keeping wages higher than they otherwise would be—there's a third very important consideration. In an open economy, not all the money made here gets spent here. Much of it finds its way abroad. And, at the same time, there's a lot more money generated in Canada from foreign sales than before. So the third consideration is this. The money spent by the welfare recipient may in fact fail to benefit a Canadian-based company. It may instead help a formidable offshore competitor, a Taiwanese toymaker, a Malaysian shirt maker or a Peruvian sweater maker, get even better. So in effect, these income maintenance programs are not only transfers from production to consumption, they represent transfers from our noncompetitive sectors to our more competitive trade partners.

It's obvious that income maintenance programs—of the kind we have now, certainly—are unaffordable at any level of economic development, because they make us worse off, not better off. When you reckon that four percent of our total goods and services are being used in this way, then you have to start worrying.

Is There a Solution?

If economics were the only consideration, the solution would be simple: stop honoring entitlements. Just end the programs. Don't supply them unless the country goes into technical recession, meaning two quarters of back-to-back decline. Politically, of course, this solution is a nonstarter. Maybe some gradual phaseouts would help. But that's not the whole story. As well, any remaining income maintenance policies, broadly speaking, ought to be linked to creating trampolines instead of traps. Trampolines like using a lump sum UI payment to start a small business that will bounce the unemployed back into the work force as rapidly as possible.

What about those who for various reasons can't really participate fully in the workforce? This group probably needs some kind of permanent assistance. But it should also be pegged to part-time work or some other useful activity. Parking people is bad —bad for the people parked. And for the rest who pay.

Rejigging these programs so that they don't discourage work will help reduce long-term unemployment. But the bill will not likely come down much. The effect will just be less inflationary, since the programs will improve the workings of job markets, not distort them. But we still haven't answered the question, "How to pay?" We're coming to that.

Eyeing the Jewel in the Crown

How could our system of medical health insurance be anything other than an entitlement program with some positive net benefits? Despite the fact we spend a little less than the United States as a proportion of our economy, our average life expectancy is a little higher. On the other hand, we spend slightly more than the Germans, and our average life expectancy is slightly lower. The amount we spend has some health improving benefits. But in fact, it appears that the age and life-styles of the people receiving the service have as much to do with the result as the amount spent. In fact, this program is more an expression of social values than economics. We believe health care is a right of citizenship and that it's most effectively supplied if the government acts as the principal coordinator of the system.

The question is how can we afford to do this? The current system actually costs $60 billion, if you include the private sector contribution of $17 billion. The problem is that these costs are now rising at about five percent a year when we're lucky to have real growth at two percent a year. So health care is affecting us structurally—the older we get, the more we transfer to the medical care sector. This situation is potentially very serious. We ought to ensure that medical health care growth stabilizes at the growth level of the economy as a whole. A lot of attention is now going into looking at controlling over-utilization through the tax system and by reallocating resources to fit demands better—more ambulatory and pharmaceutical care to free up hospital capacity for acute care use, for example.

These approaches, while laudable, don't address the main strategic aspect of the problem: as the population ages, health care is going to become an increasingly important priority for more and more of us. The health care system is like a life insurance company whose older policyholders significantly outnumber its younger policyholders.

It's clear that we need a new approach. As with income maintenance, the approach should be based on using markets, not on fighting them. One approach would be to reorganize the health care system so that the profit motive can be harnessed to slashing costs while preserving service. In a reformed system, patients' choice of doctor would drive the system even more than it does now. But the doctors would have their compensation tied to saving the system money, not costing the system money. The logic here is if we want a well-managed system, let's pay the principal actors in the system as though they were managers.

In this model, hospitals and clinics would be run as small companies in which the physicians acquire shares as they begin their careers there, have stock options available as the facility grows profitably, and can cash out as they retire. Then doctors would be inclined to find the optimum mix of service and profitability for their facility. Linking compensation to stock options would also ease pressure on the system for straight salary increases. As well, the pressures for profitability would encourage downward pressure on prices everywhere in the system.

Would this get at overuse of testing, overmedication and the resort to fashionable but relatively not cost-efficient modes of treatment? Obviously not by markets alone. The system needs a control device—one well-placed to enforce competition and use audit procedures to ensure value received. This reformed system would have two centers capable of exercising that kind of control:

• First, the patient, who would change doctors—thus affecting profitability—if the service was less than desired, and who could highlight overmedication and overtesting if he or she got suspicious. In this age of personal empowerment, people are already taking much more of an interest in their own diseases and well-being.

- Second, the buying power of the central insurer, especially in a context of competition among facilities, would offset the use of unnecessary procedures far more effectively than is now the case.

Just to underline the point, the reason the Canadian system costs less than the U.S. system is the administrative savings that arise from having single insurers with the same plans. Moreover, it wouldn't be necessary to operate every facility like this—only some. That way you could arrange competition among the different types of service providers.

But there's another strategy we could follow, too. It's apparent that life-style is a significant explanatory variable when it comes to determining life expectancy. If we focused more resources of the system on maintaining great life-styles, we'd find the demands on the system would fall off. In many businesses today, a great deal of emphasis goes to making room for fitness.

But Where's the Money Going to Come From?

One a big mistake is trying to use the tax system to finance social programs. For one thing, it limits us to the domestic financial base, which, in a global economy, is not very smart. For another, it politicizes something that's really a business matter, which conforms to known laws and principles—those of insurance.

If social programs were mutualized—that is, made into real insurance programs—the money could be raised by investing the premiums, the way other insurance is financed. That's why it's so important to get the rate of growth of hospital price increases down to the level of the growth rate—not more. Then, devising an investment strategy would be relatively easy—buying a mutual fund that covers the board would go a long way to insuring a fund growth as great or greater than the economy as a whole. As the investments mature, some borrowing would be in order.

Here's where the information economy can supply a superior solution, one that's better than what governments do now. This aspect goes a little beyond the measures we've already discussed to touch on financing. What we're really talking about when we look at these protection programs—whether of income or health—is risk. These social programs should be organized from the standpoint of risk management, and not on spurious claims to contra-cyclicity. Over the years, we've come to understand a lot about risk and society.

We now know enough to estimate with confidence the probability of a portion of the population falling into poverty and the time it takes to climb back out. The studies are widely available among social policy analysts. And a little while ago the (late) Economic Council of Canada published its application of those findings to the Canadian economy. (*The New Face of Poverty: Income Security Needs of Canadian Families.* Economic Council of Canada, 1992.) Another major development in recent years is that we've learned how to manufacture investment opportunities based on portfolio theory. We've learned that we can combine risks of different quality into packages with different risk characteristics but identical expected values.

With the aid of portfolio analysis, investors can choose between maximum returns for a given level of risk or minimum risk for a given expected return. Capital markets in an information economy are based on products created by using this kind of analysis and then sold to investors around the world. The factories of the new economy are in banks and investment houses where computers and Super Mario graduates transform credit into new financial products. The computers can retrieve the data, perform the necessary calculations at lightning speed and then can speed the new products off to likely recipients on the investment dealers' calling list.

World capital markets are broad enough and deep enough to absorb bonds based on Canada's social programs. We know enough now to construct actuarial tables of social risk for the population as a whole. Instead of financing these risks through tax, we should be able to finance them through the process known as securitization. Here's how this process would work. Canadians get a health and UIC number at birth and are expected to pay a schedule of premiums based on the known risks starting on their eighteenth birthday. And don't be misled by the idea that high-risk individuals will have to pay exorbitant premiums. Like group whole life insurance, the premium is averaged over the group. But in fact, only about a third of the population has any chance at all of falling into poverty, and of those only a few experience it at any particular time. These would be the recipients of public support. The public support would be linked to something—perhaps a retraining program or an internship with a company—that would lead to a job within a brief period. Think of the program as a kind of business.

The business result: on the income maintenance side a relatively low probability of payout in relation to a relatively high probability of a safe rate of return from premium income.

On the medicare side, with an aging population, the situation is reversed, at least at this stage of our demographic development: a relatively high probability of a substantial payout, relatively low probability of a positive rate of return, despite the reorganizations suggested a moment ago.

By combining the income maintenance offering with the health care offerings—and maybe further refining the product according to different demographic characteristics—an investment portfolio could be created. Each portfolio would be organized to meet an investor's particular strategy: maximum rate of return for given amount of risk, or minimum risk for a given rate of return. The portfolios would be launched on world capital markets. The New York Stock Exchange traded $10 trillion worth of corporate bonds in 1990. There's plenty of room for paper of the sort we're suggesting.

The money raised by the sale of these instruments would provide a steady cash flow to cover the costs of financing the income maintenance and the medicare programs. It would do so on an actuarially sound basis. With full transparency, so we could see clearly where the money was coming from and where it was going.

These are important points. Government programs—including pensions—are not yet managed on a transparent, actuarially sound basis. Uncertainty spooks investors. For the next forty years or so, the risk profile of the bonds proposed here will worsen as the baby boomers work their way from middle age to end game. Left to government, this trend will result in higher borrowing costs as risk rises relative to expected rates of return.

However, if the bonds are traded as we're suggesting, much of this could be offset by rapid, computer-assisted repackaging, essentially mixing more and more of the low risk income protection program with less and less of the health care program, and exchanging the new instruments for the old ones as the values of the older bonds fall and their yield curves climb.

This is what corporate treasuries do now. Above all, therefore, the program should be privately run—by those who will lose a lot if they make a mistake. This kind of management—as a problem in risk packaging to meet the investors' concerns about rates of return—would provide these programs with the funds they need to work properly. But the impact would go way beyond the medical and welfare sectors. Perhaps unexpectedly, tackling the problem this way would also turbocharge the Canadian economy.

One of the main benefits of mutualizing our social risk in this way is its effect on government.

If governments no longer had to raise money to keep the social system going, we could eliminate half the public sector. Maybe more. We could also cut taxes. The benefits of this would be vastly to increase the productive sector in Canada. And drastically to slice our social overheads. We would see a dramatic increase in national productivity—and therefore investment. Result: much less stress on the income maintenance programs. And so a much better risk profile for the social programs taken together.

This surge in productivity is not a byproduct. It's absolutely necessary to ensure a steady expected value of the Canada social program bonds we're proposing. For without the surge in productivity combined with full employment, not only will we not be able easily to fund our social programs: when we need the programs the most, the cupboard will, for all practical purposes, be bare. Indeed, it is bare now, as Ontario has been explaining for the last two budgets.

There's only one known technique for the kind of optimization we need to undertake to get our social programs right—let the market do it. In a global, information-based economy, the interaction of millions of personal decisions can't be sorted out any other way.

Eleven

Matters Environmental

Go, lemmings, go!

—lapel button

FAITH POPCORN, NAMESAKE of the *Popcorn Report* (on the future of your company, your world, your life) sees the 1990s as the Decency Decade—the first truly socially responsible decade. And looking after the environment is part of it. She's sure of it: "A kid prevented from playing outside because it's bad air-quality day takes air quality seriously," she says. In addition, "The predominant vision now is coming from middle age... We've taken from the world, now we want to give back. The prevailing cultural biological clock is beginning to say it's time to be good." Good.

But Canada, like almost every other industrialized country in the world, has organized its economic life as a struggle against nature, digging, cutting and gutting natural resources and then transforming them into finished or semifinished goods. We have a materialistic culture: we like things. We like the convenience they provide, their novelty and stimulation, their tangibility. Production has been geared toward satisfying what we've grown to like.

Nothing wrong with that. It's one of the defining characteristics of humans that they make tools. Ultimately you could say that all our things are tools to one end or other—tools that move us (bikes, cars, trains, planes) or tools that help us explore our imagination (toys, books, movies). Where value decisions come in is with the level of materialism we seek and what other values we're willing to forgo. Environmental deterioration is due in part to the priority we've given to improving our material well-being and our willingness to ignore the consequences of that choice.

Now the global, information economy is altering the value decisions of the developed world, and giving voice to the aspirations of the developing world that wishes to improve its material well-being, too.

It's more than coincidence that feminism has flourished and lent its values and adherents to the environmental movement in the same period as the transition to the new economy has progressed. Interdependence of relationships and, for the most part, value consensus over hierarchy and adversarial positioning are characteristics of both the global economy and the feminist philosophy. Mother Earth, despite her occasional crankiness, is becoming more appealing to modern temperaments than an angry father. At a more mundane level, it's always been the role of women in this culture to take care of things that support life at home, rather than to attend to more abstract conquests. (As an aside, women are far more suited to fit into and succeed in the information economy than they were in the industrial economy. Women have been socialized to seek compromise, be team players, shun hierarchy, network and think laterally—all the skills that are crucial to success now, and that the men who run the mature industrial corporations are struggling to master.)

Protection of the environment is now on the public agenda, not just the Canadian agenda, but the international agenda, as well. No coincidence, either, that concern about Planet Earth has paralleled the development of the new economy: deteriorating air or water quality doesn't stop at

the border, and instantaneous communication lets everyone know. Clearly, environmentalism is a new economy
thing, even though "environmentalism" means a lot of different things, and it's not always clear what "environmentalists" are trying to protect. For example, when we say
we must protect the earth, is it limited to tangibles—specific natural resources, water, gorillas? Or is it potentials—
the opportunity to discover the medicinal properties of as
yet undiscovered Amazonian plants, or the ability to provide our grandchildren with an earth that can still support
and provide for them? Is it an idea: the memory and her-
itage of a time when people still believed that the earth
was endless and our life on it indestructible? Is it a spiritual connection to the other species on the earth? Is it one
of these ends plus a means to raise other questions about
interdependence and balance: the need for more consensus, social justice, economic justice?

Whatever it is, it's pretty clear that environmental protection means we have to figure out how to produce "goods"
without creating any "bads" associated with them. Up till
recently, no one worried much about the "bads"—if a factory smokestack belches out tons of particulates that kill
trees, corrode cars and send asthmatics to the hospital, the
costs associated with that pollution aren't subtracted from
the value of the goods that go into the value of our gross
domestic product. But if the factory buys a smokestack
scrubber to stop the pollution, the value of the scrubber
pushes our GDP up. So what we want now is to figure out
two things: first, how to organize the goods production
part of our economy so that the production process is
closed—that is, nothing toxic or wasteful leaks out of it
and that the whole life cycle of the product is accounted
for; and second, how the developing world can develop
without making the same mistakes the developed world
has made.

Let's Clean Up Our Own Mess First

How our society measures our progress is the key to realizing sustainable development. All our present accounting conventions—the way we "keep score" for business and government and everything in between—fail to take into account the protection of the environment. The typical balance sheet is based on a view of the world that does not value those things that are not explicitly commercialized. The air we breathe, the water we drink, the noncommercially recoverable forest have no value unless they're organized for some kind of transaction. That may have been okay in the fifteenth century when modern accounting was developed. When there's a hole in the ozone and safe sunlight is becoming a scarce good, that approach is pretty irrelevant.

Any serious attempt to move toward sustainable development clearly implies we have to be able to account for the "bads"—in the jargon, "value external costs"—the side effects of the commercial business we do and products we make—in a standard, systematic way. Work on integrating these external costs is underway in the accounting profession. Rather less progress has been made with the problem of government accounting, in particular the national accounts.

There are a lot of suggestions around about how we might do that. Perhaps we could somehow arrange for all the resources that are now held in common, (air, oceans, rivers, mountains, forests and so on) to become someone's property, on the grounds that if you own something, you'll look after it. Perhaps we could provide a basis for better decision-making by society by making sure all resources are fully valued, (the theory being that if you undervalue a resource, you can't help but mismanage it). Perhaps we could support more worldwide institutions that will push forward a broad array of international agreements and integrate environmental objectives into other fields, such as trade and debt policy, agriculture, transportation and so on.

Along with the pursuit of all or any of these, here's another proposal that will not only go a long way toward achieving
the objectives of economic development without environmental damage, but will also position Canada as a leading
new-economy manager. The proposal is simple: replace
Finance Canada with Environment Canada as the nation's
pivotal central agency.

Environment Canada as Central Agency

At the moment, the Finance Canada is the country's central
agency, that is, it is responsible for setting economic policy and
for managing the country's financial affairs. But the new economy has rendered most of what the department does irrelevant
or meaningless. Traditional national economic policy has met
its match in the triangle of doom composed of computers,
telecommunications and financial deregulation. These allow
billions of dollars to move around the world in fractions of
seconds. World capital markets operate like a giant Nintendo
version of *The Price is Right*. And because of that, the international financial community determines real interest rates
and currency values. Thus, bond yields, stock market activity and more generally, the national supply of money and credit and economic growth are dictated to government, rather
than government dictating these to the rest of the world.

Finance Canada personnel have to pretend this isn't true,
because if they acknowledged the workings of the new
economy, they would have to seek other employment. If
Environment Canada were organized as a central agency,
it would have an answer to Finance's dilemma: simply
accept the fact that the international economy and the private sector's response to it will determine economic growth.
Instead let's say to ourselves, here's how our economic
activity will affect the environment over a fiscal year; let's
see how positive we can afford to make the effect. The

idea is to stop using the tax system in a mainly useless effort to steer national economic activity, and instead use it to steer national environmental benignity.

Environment Canada (instead of Finance Canada) would work with Statistics Canada to prepare the national accounts. It would work with Revenue Canada to ensure we have an environmentally benign tax system. For instance, carbon and other emission taxes would go to funds for developing closed technology, for which tax credits would be possible. It would work with the industrial departments to ensure we had environmentally benign industries. Tax credits or even transfer payments could be available for certain environmentally friendly policies—increasing the gene pool in agriculture, introducing more effective waste treatment and so on. These policies would result in lower environment degradation, which would help preserve book values of certain types of assets, leading to lower borrowing rates for loans they secure, and so on. Environment Canada would also ensure that the funding of income maintenance came out of investment funds that helped make Canada a world leader in certain environmentally benign resource technologies.

Maybe you think this picture is farfetched. Clearly an Environment Canada central agency would not be the Environment Canada we have now. For this "vision" to occur, one very big change would have to happen. Environment Canada would have to be able to exert intellectual leadership. And the department's perspective would have to broaden correspondingly.

Up to now Environment Canada has functioned like a nun in a boarding school—looking for sinful emissions. There've been some notable successes, especially in long-range airborne pollutants and acid rain. From the provincial buy-in to a common emission-reduction target to the recent conclusion of a Canada-U.S. treaty, the department has played an internationally recognized leadership role. But it still takes a kind of law-enforcement perspective. And successful cities don't put traffic cops in charge of traffic policy. Moving environment to center stage will require the department to dump enforcement and get better at putting the policy choices before the country.

Some of this is occurring. Environment Canada is in the process of moving the enforcement function out of the department—although the new agency still lacks the administrative teeth of the Environmental Protection Agency in the United States. And, just as Finance has its economists, Environment Canada has a body of expert opinion against which its policies can be tested. Environmental groups are divided, it's true, but when were economists any different? Environmentalists are no longer running in the streets—instead they are grouping themselves into think tanks where they undertake policy-relevant research. These environmental groups can be the leverage points for building influential coalitions. And like economists with respect to other economic sectors, the environmentalists can act as catalysts—moving the other stakeholders toward agreement or compromise.

But as this occurs, Environment Canada will have to be ready to work with these other stakeholders, showing them how environmental friendliness is congruent with business success. One way for Environment Canada to do this is to be able to propose a tax system based on sustainable development, rather than on the value of real estate or income. Maybe the Canadian Tax Foundation and the Canadian Institute of Chartered Accountants could collaborate to figure out a financial management system based on environmental benignity.

Environment Canada will have to lead a national discussion of this issue. It must have its own experts capable of interacting on this file with other external experts. It must develop this expertise within business associations. Many of these associations are already developing ideas. But they have no place to take them— Finance isn't interested, and Environment Canada at the moment isn't properly positioned. But the possibility is there for Environment Canada to appropriate the coalition that now sees Finance as its chief link with public policy.

That's the role Environment Canada could play if it was capable of replacing Finance as a central agency. And if it was capable of working with environmental organizations to come up with a fiscal framework appropriate to sustainable development.

A Proposal to Address the Developing World

Here's the problem: the developing world wants the stuff the developed world has. It wants development so its inhabitants can live a better quality material life. Developing countries are much more dependent than industrial and information countries on their natural resources. But so many people are so poor that they are cutting down trees for fuel, farming on soil that is too fragile to support them, and in general destroying their resource base. All because they have no options. And now we know that destruction of the world's tropical forests also hurts the planet's greatest storehouse of biological diversity, which affects our well-being, too.

So here's one way to give the developing world some options other than digging, cutting and gutting: ensure that developing countries can make and trade knowledge-based products. As things are going today, the GATT and North American Free Trade Agreement (NAFTA) negotiations are being framed by a world based on the old industrial economy. Mass production. Economies of scale. Mass markets. These markets send assembly jobs to cheap labor countries. They encourage mines and forests and single-crop commodity production as the main exports. While this is happening, most of the innovation capacity will stay in the north.

The resulting trade patterns will generally be that G-7 nations will all pursue high value-added manufacturing of complex products for global market niches. That knowledge will be transferred to assembly undertaken in the south. The finished products will be exported from the south. But technology transfer will be limited to that contained in production machinery. In other words, the effect will likely be to restrict the participation of low- and middle-income countries in the knowledge economy except as consumers of technology developed elsewhere. From an environmental standpoint, these arrangements are probably a mistake, because any arrangement that slows down the distribution of knowledge-based production will do little to help the developing world develop benignly. What's more, these assembly countries lack the institutional strength to force zero-discharge production on their factories.

Participation in the knowledge economy would mean that the incentive for commodity production was starkly reduced. Instead, the pressure would be on to find things of higher new value to supply to world markets. There's no shortage of knowledge to be developed in the rain forest. There's a shortage of qualified scientists. Cutting down trees is a reasonable choice only in restricted circumstances. Nor should agricultural production encourage soil exhaustion. Rather there's every reason to preserve fertility, except in special circumstances. In a knowledge economy, there's every reason to develop new, knowledge-intensive bioproducts—herbs, medicines, pharmaceuticals with high value added. Add to this the incentives associated with mastering aspects of environmentally clean production. That's an exportable product or service.

Basically, our trade arrangements either restrict participation in the knowledge economy or insist that it be conducted according to special rules that favor the migration of declining developed-world industrial sectors to regions that have the weakest environmental defenses. Why? Because the GATT and NAFTA arrangements reflect the powerful bargaining interest of declining sectors, not the global aspirations of new sectors. It's the auto industries that want to transfer labor-intensive production to Mexico. It's the giant commodity producers who want free market entry and domestic subsidies. And it's the International Monetary Fund and the banking sector that are seeking official guarantees to stave off the bank closings that other businesses suffer after they've made major mistakes. Driving all this are industrial concepts of mass production and mass markets. The declining sectors make up in political clout what they're losing economically. So it's not surprising that trade talks should proceed on the basis of what was rather than what is.

In the trade talks being negotiated, the new economy drivers (telecommunciations, areospace, medical technology) are generally not in the driver's seat. Indeed, telecommunications will be subject to special protections. Aerospace will be carefully managed. Medical technology will generally be developed in northern labs, not southern. In practice, trade "liberalization" is about prolonging the life cycle of declining sectors not about internationalizing new ones. Therefore, it's the other, more politically powerful but older sectors that are grudgingly forced to liberalize, albeit along carefully drawn lines. The environmental problem arises from the fact that liberalizing these old sectors puts stress on the environment. This wouldn't occur if we worked as hard to liberalize the new sectors and to transform the older ones.

Getting There

To generalize from the main thrust of this chaper, what matters is how you look at things. Through an industrial lens, "sustainablility" looks very dark indeed, fraught with controls, restrictions and expensive add-ons. But if we put on some post-industrial glasses, then "sustainable development" seems a lot easier to achieve.

The key is accepting that a knowledge-based economy lets us do a lot of things differently. If we really want to make sustainability a top priority, then we can let our government structure reflect our central concern.

As well, according to this perspective, the industrialized world should stop trying to reproduce yesterday's industries in the southern tier of countries. Instead, the rich countries should adopt a strategy that recognizes their comparative advantage in environmental enforcement and strive to get developing countries into environmentally friendly, knowledge-based industries as soon as possible.

That might be easier than you'd think. Perhaps surprisingly, there's not much of a problem transferring knowledge and upgrading the technical capabilities in middle-income and other countries. Anybody with a computer and a modem can communicate around the world—or at least around the world's major technology centers, often for the price of a local phone call. And privatization of phone companies in those countries will generally improve the phone service sufficiently.

The simplest way to induce the liberalization of the new sector would be to introduce some kind of General Preference Tariff System for knowledge-based products, so that the knowledge component of any product made in a country to which the general preference system applied would be allowed into an advanced country duty-free. Combined with the telecom revolution, it's not hard to envisage the result. Raw science from all over the world would flow into those countries, to be developed and commercialized into new templates and designs for shipment to assembly points elsewhere—in advanced countries with the capacity to protect the environment.

Then, instead of cutting down the rain forests, it would make more sense to husband its species. And instead of over-farming a fragile topsoil, more effort would go into creating new seeds and other bioengineering activity.

To get there, though, we have to be able to look at things with fresh eyes, in a new way, and see things the way they are—not the way they used to be.

Part 3

Excelling at Alice's Croquet

Alice thought she had never seen such a curious croquet-ground in all her life: it was all ridges and furrows: the croquet balls were all hedgehogs, and the mallets live flamingos, and the soldiers had to double themselves up and stand on their hands and feet, to make the arches.

The chief difficulty Alice found at first was in managing her flamingo: she succeeded in getting its body tucked away, comfortably enough, under her arm, with its legs hanging down, but generally, just as she got its neck nicely straightened out, and was going to give the hedgehog a blow with its head, it would twist itself round and look up in her face, with such a puzzled expression that she could not help bursting out laughing; and, when she got its head down, and was going to begin again, it was very provoking to find that the hedgehog had unrolled itself, and was in the act of crawling away: besides all this, there was generally a ridge or a furrow in the way wherever she wanted to send the hedgehog to, and, as the doubled-up soldiers were always getting up and walking off to other parts of the ground, Alice concluded that it was a very difficult game indeed.

—Alice's Adventures in Wonderland,
by Lewis Carroll

ALICE'S CROQUET HAS become the metaphor for how we're living our lives today: nothing is stable for very long, everything is alive and changing, the rules we understood yesterday have given way today to new rules or, in some cases, no rules. Robert Kriegel, whom *U.S. News and World Report* describes as "a leading authority in the field of human performance," points out that "the overnight letter, which was the speed innovation of the eighties, is now used only when you're not in a hurry." Kriegel's latest book, *If It Ain't Broke... BREAK IT!*, puts a twist on as much conventional wisdom as he could find: "Rip-roaring, nerve-shattering change means we cannot rely on the 'tried and true', because what was tried yesterday is no longer true today."

In the course of interviewing a hundred or so Canadians who are playing Alice's croquet, and winning, we found similar attitudes and approaches, no matter how different the people and the professions. The handful of profiles and experiences coming up are, as were the suggested answers for change in Part Two, meant to whet your appetite, to help you think in other directions about your own attitudes to work and living, and how you might get big rewards from taking risks and making changes.

Twelve

Doing It

Michael Cowpland, President,
Corel Systems Corporation

WITH LANGUAGE ONE of the few barriers left in a global economy, now more than ever a picture is worth the proverbial thousand words. Michael Cowpland, president of Corel Systems Corporation of Ottawa, says the rapid advancement of his company is proof that the old maxim applies. His firm's graphics software program, Corel Draw!, is produced in twenty-one different language versions, sells to some fifty countries and is regarded by many as the world standard in its domain.

A mark of Corel Draw!'s reach is the response to an international art contest Corel holds every year for users. In one year, the number of entries went from seven hundred to three thousand with submissions coming from thirty-five countries.

"You don't have to explain pictures," Cowpland says of the remarkable success he has enjoyed since he founded Corel in 1985. "Graphics are truly international. You can understand them equally as well in Russian as you can in English."

Certainly, a Corel Draw! pie chart of Corel's accomplishments would tell an encouraging story about Canadian entrepreneurship. Annual revenues at Cowpland's seven-year-old firm are more than $50 million, and the company's growth rate has been a phenomenal seventy percent a year.

Significantly, more than ninety percent of Corel's business is done outside Canada's borders. About half those sales are to the United States and more than the remaining half are to companies and individuals around the world.

"A complete spectrum of clients use Corel Draw!" says Cowpland, an engineer himself who was doing computer chip design as early as 1970. "There are six-year-olds in Holland using it to make art, there are businesses all over using it for presentations—even sign cutters use it. And it's been proven that you retain up to five times more with graphics than when you use ordinary linear communication. The process calls for whole brain communication as opposed to just left brain—and that's what's helped make our product so universal. The program is right at the boundary of art and technology."

Cowpland's success is particularly sweet after the fate of his last venture, Mitel Corporation of Kanata, Ontario. Mitel was regarded as a comer in telecommunications equipment when it arrived on the scene in the early seventies. But after an extraordinary period of growth—stocks in the company more than quadrupled in value shortly after they were issued—profits suddenly started to plummet. The problem: too much plant capacity and mounting cost overruns. In short order, the firm closed facilities and laid off hundreds of employees, and in 1986, Cowpland left the company he had founded.

But rather than being cowed by the rise and fall of Mitel, Cowpland took to heart the lessons he'd learned—and made the transition necessary for doing business in the new economy. While he was still prepared to gamble on an enterprise with promise, he did so on his own terms and in his own way. That meant keeping a handle on the size of his staff and not relying on lenders for support. Today, Corel has about 250 employees—scant compared to the many hundreds he employed in the Mitel days. What's more, the new company is debt-free.

"I didn't have any qualms about starting Corel despite what happened," says Cowpland. "I'd made a ton of money at Mitel and was interested in getting into something else. I put $7 million of my personal cash into Corel over a period of about four years."

Corel particularly avoids government funding, although there is much money to be had in grants for companies such as his that are actively involved in high-tech research and development. "We don't want it because it takes too long to get it and involves so much paperwork," he says with the maverick attitude that marks most successful Canadian entrepreneurship. He adds that, if anything, the government has proven a source of frustration for his firm in terms of customs regulations. "Even under free trade, customs staff act like policemen," he maintains. "They certainly don't seem to be there to help business. By their attitude, you'd think we're trying to clamp down on trade—not free it up."

Despite such annoyances, Corel has flourished, in part because of Cowpland's move to make Corel Draw! function with Windows 3.0, Microsoft's smash best-selling operating system. But in reality, it was a series of canny decisions that sent Corel into the stratosphere.

"We didn't have a grand vision," he maintains. "I think when you launch a business, you never know how it's going to end up because you have to optimize all the way along. The key is to start in a field that has growth potential, and to continuously tune your product as you go."

Since the Mitel experience, Cowpland has learned to make changes quickly—adapting his company to immediately respond to potential markets and new products. Corel, in fact, started out in hardware, with systems integration as a principal focus. But the company moved away from the field as better and more challenging opportunities presented themselves.

"We managed the change without any write-offs although we had to close down a third of the company," he says. "But we chose to move into desktop systems because it was a new area of innovation in computers—even we had to learn as we went along. These days, everybody has to roll with the punches. At this juncture, it's impossible to have a master plan in business—to predict even five years ahead. If someone could do that, they'd have been hired by IBM or General Motors long ago, and those companies wouldn't be in the trouble they're in today."

What Cowpland values most about his firm now is the staff atmosphere. He insists on the active interchange of ideas with all his employees.

"I think it's great to have free-flowing brainstorming," he says about the way his personnel bandy about concepts and proposals. "On the whole, people like to bounce ideas around, and I like to encourage them. We don't even know who's responsible for most of our ideas because we don't really pay attention to where they're coming from when we brainstorm. No one person is the author of an idea, because somewhere along the way, it has to be transformed and optimized. That's why I'm against formal employee suggestion plans, because [those kinds of incentives] force you to build a little wall around an idea, put someone's name on it like a label and associate a dollar value with it. That can stunt flexibility."

His encouragement and his quick response to suggestions from the floor have resulted in some pretty happy corporate campers. In a recent employee survey, staff rated job satisfaction at 99.5%, compared to the Canadian average of about 35%. It gives him confidence that his troops will be behind him whichever direction his company takes in the near future.

"We want to be in more or less the same field," he says of his plans for Corel down the road. "We've carved ourselves out a mandate: to be the number one graphics supplier for computers in the world. That may lead us into animation and other forms of multimedia. At the moment it's not clear, because it never is. We just know that right now, we want

Corel Draw! on every computer. And we're on our way to accomplishing that."

Leonard Lee, President, Lee Valley Tools (Canada), Veritas Tools (U.S.)

After fourteen years with the federal government, Ottawa's Leonard Lee might have been content to live out his life as a career civil servant in Ottawa. From his first job as a vice consul in Chicago with the Canadian Foreign Service to his last with the Department of Industry, Trade and Commerce, he had security and status and was moving up the ranks.

Then he got gripped by what he describes as a mid-life crisis, leaving the government at the age of forty in 1978 and starting his own business manufacturing woodworking tools.

If only more Canadians had mid-life crises like his. In just fourteen years, his company has grown from 2 employees to 150 and is marketing successfully all over the world. "I think insanity grabs men when they find that they're losing their hair." He laughs, describing his decision to set up his own shop in the cutthroat worlds of manufacturing and retailing. "Most men I know just go berserk in their late thirties and early forties. I avoided that. But I did need a change."

He was also reacting to the fact that working for government had taken a turn for the worse since he had come on board in 1963. "Used to be that you felt you could achieve a great deal in government. There was more individual responsibility and fewer layers of management to contend with," he recalls. "When I joined the Department of Industry, Trade and Commerce, there were fewer than three hundred people in it and I knew every one of them. When I left, there were nearly three thousand and I knew fewer than when I had joined. The government had become very large and just didn't have the sense of focus or purpose that it originally had."

What made the plunge easier for him was strong spousal support. "Since woodworking was my hobby, I did market research in my spare time and saw what I thought was a tidy small market in specialist woodworking tools. My wife just said, 'The worst you could do is go broke—and that's four thousand dollars ahead of where we were when we got married.' "

When his findings turned up the fact that woodworking hobbyists made up about five percent of the Canadian population, he was convinced he could make a go of the business. To keep costs down, he opted for a mail-order approach, although his first Ottawa warehouse was also a retail outlet. Then he made a critical decision—to provide potential customers with high-quality catalogues full of detail and information. One ad in the magazine *Harrowsmith* generated a request for more than two thousand copies of the catalogue, and he was launched. The rest may be history, but it's also a blueprint for the future of Canadian entrepreneurship.

To some extent, though, Lee is bucking the trend in Canadian business at the end of the twentieth century. At a time when many new ventures are finding success marketing software or telecommunications equipment, his field is manufacturing—and relatively low-tech manufacturing, at that. His principal business philosophy is to treat the customer like a friend. But while his products may be folksy and his approach down-home, he's using the kind of highly sophisticated service techniques that mark the new entrepreneur. Among his policies: strong technical service and support for his products. He's dedicated half his customer service department to providing technical help to clients—information on where to buy items, on problem solving, even on how to work with tools his firm doesn't make.

"We'll also reward customers when they save us trouble," he says. "A customer came into our Ottawa showroom with a honing guide he'd bought from us [that] wasn't working.

As soon as I saw it in action I knew what was wrong. We had more than fourteen hundred of these products in the hands of dealers, all in the United States and Europe. Fortunately we got them all shipped back. The customer who brought this to our attention got a hundred dollars worth of gifts, since he saved us money."

Right now, about ninety-five percent of his exports go to the United States, with sales picking up in Britain and Europe. But he's always conscious of his customers and their needs, wherever they live. For example, Canadian market research shows that the typical woodworker is a male hobbyist with a basement workshop. If Lee had totally bought into that research, he'd have had a hard time selling his products in Europe, where homes traditionally don't have basements.

"The lesson here," he said recently, "is to know your market. Success in Canada doesn't guarantee sales abroad. We do everything we can to eliminate borders. We don't come across as foreign. At the very least, we aim to be as good as domestic suppliers—and preferably better. We want our foreign customers to feel warm and secure."

It rankles Lee that small business in Canada has to contend with mounds of regulation and paperwork—obstacles to getting the job done and keeping the profits mounting.

"There's a ferocious deadweight of regulatory control that exists in this country," he contends. "It's just impossible for a small business to meet all the various regulations, whether they deal with tax reporting, permits or whatever. The administrative load is punitive. And when you consider that people starting small businesses have to take financial risks—often putting their life savings on the line—the atmosphere mitigates the development of small business. We don't have the right climate."

Perhaps because he has insight into the inner workings of government, he's not the least bit intimidated at the thought of tackling some of these regulations head on. He has tilted at windmills—and they have tilted back.

Recently, he lobbied against a federal order that allowed packages valued at forty dollars or less mailed to Canada from other countries to be exempted from all duties and taxes. "The order was designed so that a granny sending a toy to a grandchild in Canada wouldn't have to pay these taxes," he explains. "But it was having a real effect on us. Mail-order houses were shipping to Canada without having to pay duties or manufacturers' sales tax or provincial sales tax. That put us at a substantial disadvantage. So I went to the government and said: 'Look what this loophole is doing to us. The $40 limit should be reduced because it's a substantial disadvantage to Canadian firms.' "

The government argued that it was actually just about to raise the exemption to $100, because the people who used the duty remission order had been finding it too low. "I said to the feds: 'this shouldn't be a news flash. When you ask Canadians if they want to pay fewer taxes, they're bound to say yes. But they're not the people affected.' I turned up the heat as the build-up in exempted parcels went from $5 million to something like $34 million last year. The whole thing was becoming an issue. Now they're lowering the limit from $40 to $20 and applying some specific changes to counterbalance what the United States does. I feel the only way the government will react is if you pressure them. It seems to be single-issue politics these days. You make your issue hot and they'll react."

His victory in that area prompted him to think about taking on other government regulations he found restrictive. "A couple of years ago, I started lobbying the government to undertake the regulatory review required under the free trade agreement," he says. "By 1997 we'll have to have harmonized standards and regulations when we completely reach free trade. But government still hasn't been looking at the competitive effects of standards and regulations." He wrote four articles on the subject for the Ottawa *Citizen* in which he laid out all his concerns in print. "By then I had sharpened my lance and was charging off in all directions—many of which had little to do with my own business but all of which had to do with the competitive climate in Canada. Since then, regulatory review has become a cause célèbre."

Increasingly, successful Canadian entrepreneurs are renaissance people. Their concerns extend beyond the narrow bottom line of their own profits—they recognize their businesses can only truly thrive in a healthy world. Lee fits the mold. He's a member of the Woodworkers Alliance for Rainforest Protection—a group devoted to issues such as sustainable yield in forestry. A great advocate for change, he's one for not resting on his laurels and settling in for the long term. "I tell the staff all the time that I always want the customer to have a sense of wonder. I want my clients to be thinking, 'I wonder where these guys get these ideas from, how they develop this stuff.' There has to be some sense of anticipation among your customer base of what's coming next."

Low-tech or high-tech, the theme of movement, change, adaptability, evolution and loving what you do persists.

Glenn Farrell, President and CEO; Lucille Pacey, Vice President, Technology and Educational Television; Open Learning Agency

If you can open your mind to the world, you can be as comfortable in the global village as you are in your own neighborhood.

For people like Glenn Farrell and Lucille Pacey, that's a working philosophy. The two Canadians, extremely conscious of the paradigm shift from manufacturing to knowledge in Canadian business, have assumed the daunting task of harnessing the driving force behind the new economy—education. Together, they've set unique standards at British

Columbia's Open Learning Agency (OLA), arguably the world's most innovative knowledge institution.

Founded in 1988 as part of British Columbia's public education system, OLA enrolls more than twenty thousand people a year by providing the chance to study from home, at work or in local centers. The facility was set up because people like Farrell and Pacey recognized that distance learning, with ten million students around the globe, is the fastest-growing segment of education in the world. Distance education literally and figuratively knows no boundaries.

OLA works because it takes advantage of all the latest technology available for getting information and training to its clients. Using techniques such as satellite and computer teleconferencing and telecommunications equipment, OLA's three hundred employees deliver college, university and adult and general education courses to all takers, wherever they are.

"It was already clear to me, as far back as the early seventies, that this was the route to go," says Farrell, who serves as president and CEO of the Open Learning Agency. "I realized that new technologies involving TV, radio and computers were coming on the scene—and that these were all ways to enable people to get access to the skills and knowledge they needed whatever their focus. So my career evolved along those lines."

Farrell started out with a degree in animal science and with the objective of holding workshops on nutrition, animal breeding and so on for farmers and ranchers. In the early sixties, he worked for a CBC program called *Farm Radio Forum* out of Saskatchewan, which discussed agricultural techniques and innovations.

"One of my earliest assignments," he recalls, "was to help organize community groups and arrange the distribution of print materials that the CBC produced to go along with the show. People would gather around the radio in farm kitchens and use the print material to have discussions afterward. I remember thinking how much more use we could make of radio—and that helped point me in the direction I'm now in."

OLA sees as its mandate nothing less than affording all British Columbians the opportunity to keep learning and honing skills throughout their lives.

"Our approach is that what we take on, we want to do well," he says. "We're very much involved in the process of being a quality organization. We put the learners first and try to react to their needs."

Pacey, who is OLA's vice president of technology and educational television, echoes the sentiment that learners must be the priority in any educational institution. She was a teacher before she took on her role with OLA, and she says she discovered first hand in the classroom how important it was to be flexible for her students. "I never wanted to be a teacher, but I ended up in a classroom anyway," she says. "My bias was that I had to be involved in activities that were nontraditional. Sometimes the kind of specified, rigid schedule you find in the classroom is better suited to the instructors or the institution itself than it is to the students. Also, I was more interested in working with people who had an experience base, rather than with youngsters. And all that eventually led me to OLA."

Pacey says the institution has had to overcome some equally rigid thinking on the part of the general public. "People tend to think of distance learning as a marginal activity," she says. "We have to spend a lot of time and energy proving that what we do is as good as what happens in any traditional institution. And I think we've wasted a lot of time as a result. It's been difficult for us to help governments understand what goes on with a distance college—because they can't see it. When they go to a regular college, they visit a physical facility, they walk through hallways, they see students in a classroom. We hook our students up through telephone lines or hold audio conferences, and government officials say: 'Gee, I'm not very comfortable with this. I don't know what's happening.' "

Bringing decision-makers along until they recognize the value of organizations such as the Open Learning Agency can be frustrating, say Farrell and Pacey. "I get impatient at the degree to which educational systems are comprehending the art of the possible," Farrell says. "I think educational broadcast is one of the most powerful media that we've ever developed— and we just have to use these kinds of approaches more effec- tively than we already have. What's more, as Canadians, we'd better stake out our own turf. I don't mean we should put up electronic barriers at the border, but it seems to me we should be doing more than sitting back and being recipients of infor- mation. We should be generating more of it ourselves. And there's an international market for education. As we create quality products, we could participate in that market."

One of the most interesting aspects of OLA is, in fact, its market-driven approach to learning. "Most educational insti- tutions plan their provision of services based on demand," says Pacey. "We've turned that around and started looking at the labor market from the supply side of the equation. From that, and from analyzing what we think will happen in British Columbia in the future in terms of changing jobs and require- ments for additional education, we've been able to come up with some fairly tight figures that show us very clearly that we won't have enough young people to fill the jobs required."

One statistic of particular interest: Pacey says figures show people will have to be retrained about five times during the course of their careers. She believes that the business sector will have to assume a lot of the responsibility for that retrain- ing. "That's why we've created a workplace training team," she explains. "It's a business unit that moves out to other organizations to train personnel."

The extraordinary flexibility of learning settings OLA encourages will result in a citizenship of global thinkers. To promote the broad base of knowledge required, Farrell envisions creating what amount to learning pods throughout Canada and the world. "I think OLA will be an active player in the development of community-based learning centers," he says of where he thinks the institution is heading. "They may happen within work communities or at neighborhood facilities. But the idea would be that people could go there and participate in learning opportunities of a wide variety. Much of it will be done with two-way communication technology—interactive computer and voice networks, interactive video, interactive text. And one of the hallmarks of this sort of thing will be the international nature of some of the programming. I imagine, for example, study circles perhaps focusing on some aspect of the environment. We could link them up throughout the world."

That could mean that a globally linked knowledge pool helping solve international problems is on the verge of reality.

Marti Smye, President,
People Tech Consulting Inc.

When you have to inflict a cut to remove a problem, it's best to have a physician at your side. Marti Smye is a change doctor who is spearheading a highly profitable business helping companies adapt to new realities. In fact her company, the Toronto-based People Tech, is really a trauma clinic for business—a multifaceted consulting agency that helps corporate clients recover and profit from mergers, acquisitions and restructuring. She's also there for firms undergoing technological innovations, deregulation, shifting business strategies and legislative blockades.

Smye is recently back from Prague, where People Tech is getting a toehold in the newly opened eastern European market. And if ever there was a time to manage change, it's certainly now, in the former Iron Curtain countries that are striving to move from planned to market economies. She's the kind of businesswoman who has the foresight to go beyond Canadian boundaries if that's where the opportunities lie.

"If you're in the change management business," she points out, "you should be where the action is—where the change is so dramatic."

But Smye says the need for change in corporate North America, while less striking, is just as pronounced. And corporate North America apparently agrees. Her sales for 1992 are an estimated $5.7 million and will likely go higher with her recently opened offices in Prague and Boston. The field of change management is relatively new, and it reflects the inter-disciplinary approach many companies now recognize they need in order to embark on a radically different business style.

Smye does more than hold the hands of her charges. "I'm not interested in change for change's sake," she stresses. "We're results-oriented. We create integrated action plans that combine communication, critical skill and behavior training, job definitions and employee recognition programs. We get all the employees involved to learn change management skills."

Smye, who has a PhD in psychology from the University of Toronto, got in on the ground floor with People Tech, a simple human resources firm, which she joined in 1977. But it was her far-thinking approach that has pushed her company to the front of the line in its field. She originally had two partners, but she bought out her last partner two years ago, recognizing that a company with only one concentration and a limited view would have restricted success in the new economy. "I had this vision," she says of her decision. "I knew I wanted to bring a variety of different disciplines to the task of helping our clients. And I had to go it alone in order to pursue that vision. I guess I see a lot of opportunity where others see pain or fear."

She credits her parents with giving her the sense of confidence to sidestep the safe route and follow her instincts. "Was

I scared at the outset? Absolutely," admits Smye, who grew up on a farm in Ohio. "The adrenaline is running every day. But my parents were entrepreneurs. They drove me to high standards. I own seventy percent of this business and now have three other partners who each own ten percent of the company. Just recently we had all our parents together at a dinner to thank them for giving us the courage to take risks. What's interesting is that each of us had entrepreneurial parents."

Smye and her team of twenty-six pyschologists and consultants are hired by CEOs who are often trying to cope with massive layoffs. She finds that she runs up against certain mind-sets in helping them adjust to restructuring. "CEOs tend to fall into three distinct categories," she explains. "There are the kind who think they ought to be able to handle the changes themselves—and they're our number one obstacle. There are others who don't have vision and aren't really interested in executing change; they're hanging on by their fingernails. The third kind share our vision; they're innovative, they want our support and they'll help create a team that People Tech can be part of. Of course, we work best when CEOs really believe in me—when they believe in my vision and get behind it."

Often, she says, her hardest task is helping middle managers who actually have to fire their workers; not only do they experience a sense of loss, but they frequently feel they weren't part of the decision-making process. And they wonder whether the next bullet has their name on it.

But if some companies are dragged toward change kicking and screaming, more and more are realizing that evolving to meet the new marketplace is essential to remaining competitive. Among her clients: IBM Canada Ltd., Metropolitan Life Assurance and the R.J. Reynolds Company. She adds that firms that let her company help can allay the shock of change in more ways than one. "There's a lot of anxiety and stress involved in restructuring," she emphasizes. "When it happens, companies are tampering with their dreams, their futures and their hopes—and you can never take away all the pain. But you can ease it and dissipate it away more quickly."

And then there's the bottom line. "One client told us that compared to an earlier effort, we saved them five months of time and lots of dollars," she says. "And if we ever knew how many dollars, our bill would probably be higher."

Lobbyist Susan Murray, who met Smye through a mutual client, characterizes Smye as a leader in her field. "She takes a company and looks at where they want to be in a decade," says Murray. "She questions what they need in the domestic market to make them competitive globally, and that's what's helped her build her firm into one of the largest of its kind in Canada. She's the ultimate professional—a risk taker, with boundless optimism." Smye says that optimism is just good business practice.

"My business is my work, my hobby, my fun," she says. "And if you don't have a dream yourself, you can't expect the people who work for you to be excited about coming in every day. They have to dream with you. Everybody who works here wants us to have $40 million in sales by the year 2000. But it's not for the billable hours or the salary. We're committed to change—to getting real performance for our clients. That's where the source of the excitement is."

Pierre Marc Johnson,
Centre for Medicine, Ethics and Law,
McGill University

In his forty-five years, Pierre Marc Johnson has lived several lifetimes. He served as premier of Quebec in 1985 under the Parti Québecois government and led the opposition for two years after that. During his career as a politician, between 1976 and 1987, he also held several senior ministerial posts, among them: intergovernmental affairs; justice; social development; labor and manpower.

He came equipped for each task. What few people realize is that aside from the expected degree in political science, Johnson holds degrees in medicine and law—and has practised both. Nowadays, he's a member of McGill University's famed multidisciplinary Centre for Medicine, Ethics and Law. As well, he's an international consultant on the environment, who recently served as a special adviser to conference leader Maurice Strong at the Rio summit.

All this broad education and experience has served him well as someone at the vanguard of transitional times. "When I got out of politics," says Johnson, who also practices law with the Quebec firm Guy & Gilbert in Montreal and teaches the subject at McGill, "I found I needed to address issues that were personally and intellectually satisfying. When you've been minister of social affairs or of justice and when you've headed the government even for a short time, you deal with substantive issues. Then when you go back to private life, the idea of selling peas becomes a source of anxiety."

There was little question that selling peas would ever become his fate. But he was debating which of his many intellectual interests he would turn to when two incidents affected his decision. First, he took a seminal trip to Southeast Asia with a friend. He brought Gro Brundtland's now-famous environmental report *Our Common Future* to read along the way. That and the trip to Thailand and Burma served as personal turning points.

He was struck by the contrasts he saw there. On the one hand, he says, Bangkok looked like Toronto or Montreal looked in the fifties and sixties. On the other hand, the Burmese temples he visited had remained untouched for six hundred years. It got him questioning how development and the environment affected each other.

"The second thing that decided my direction was a conference I gave at McGill on environmental issues. I'd been asked to do so because the students knew the issue interested me. I said yes and totally forgot that I hadn't appeared in public in a year. And on the news that night it was reported that I was now involved in the environment. It propelled me," he recalls. The die was cast.

He had already been offered several positions in the health field, but he demurred. "I felt I would regress," he said of the narrow focus he feared would result. "I didn't want to have to go to an office and criticize parts of the regulations I'd written myself five years before. Besides, I felt instinctively the environment would become a major issue—not only socially and in terms of values. It would change society."

In short order, he found himself conscripted by the federal government to sit on a committee preparing for a G-7 summit that was to be held in Paris in 1989. "I hesitated, because I was still pretty new to the subject," he says. "But I decided to go. I wound up in a room with three experts from each country and twelve people from the European community. I also learned in the weeks before the meeting that there were going to be three Nobel prize winners around the table. You can bet I worked on my text a lot."

His involvement in the area of environment has also helped inform his global view of politics and economics. He takes a strong position that the Western world is going to be dramatically shaken by advancement in some of the developing countries.

He says television has had a tremendous impact on the world, providing information and images to people in all corners of the globe. But he adds that the other major agent of globalization is business. "The greatest linkers of continents used to be the intellectuals," he maintains, "the professors who went to seminars in Europe a few times a year. But nowadays, business people go ten or fifteen times a year. It's a big, big shift in who's linking the world together. Business tends to be more democratic. If you're good, you can compete and succeed. And when the major corporations of the world decided it would be best to open all markets, a great deal resulted from that. Barriers began to come down between countries. Major extractors wanted resources and major producers wanted to open up world trade. That's been going on for twenty years. But it's still a phenomenon of the elite. The big question—and the challenge—is the extent to which that globalization will affect the larger population."

That means, says Johnson, that the West is going to have to equip itself for massive change. "The Western world had better get its act together," he contends. "Because Japan, China and India are starting to. South Americans also are trying to build middle classes and market economies, and they're beginning to accept that the military won't do everything. These are gigantic places and gigantic market forces and they can generate a lot of wealth. But at the same time, those who will carry the wealth won't have the same kind of historical views we have—they won't even have the same God, in many cases. That's going to have a profound impact on legal systems and social relationships."

He says Canada would be wise to align itself to Europe as these changes begin to take place. "We can't handle the concerns of the Western world by sticking only with what the Americans think and do," he argues. "It won't work. It was possible until the age of communications and globalization. But in reality, only about twenty percent of the world has its roots in the Age of Enlightenment, in Adam Smith, in social democracies and Judeo-Christianity. And eighty percent of the world comes from a different background. As that world develops, the changes are going to affect everybody's daily lives in twenty years from now."

It's a message he's trying to convey to his own two teenagers whom he is trying to prepare for the new world order. "I advise them that education is fundamentally important," he stresses. "Their generation isn't going to have it easy. Mine had everything going for it. The sixties were exciting times. There were jobs, and there was a lot of speculating on land going on in North America. They also missed the fast-buck speculative economy of the eighties. But by the time my kids grow up, we'll have rendered this continent a garbage bin in certain areas. We'll have over-fished and increased atmospheric pollution. At the same time, we'll be telling them to pay for our old age. And why should they? Sure, I love what I do and the adrenaline is very high. But one of the reasons I'm involved in these issues is that I feel they're relevant to my kids."

Like so many movers in the new economy, Johnson is loath to predict what he'll be doing down the road. "In five years, I'm quite sure I won't be doing what I'm doing now," he guesses. "That's the only certainty I have. Right now, I'm too spread out. Maybe I'll find myself a niche and specialize—become the best in the world at what I do. Then maybe I'll have more time to write. Or maybe I'll go back to politics. But then—" he laughs "—I'm not sure I'd have time to think."

Jim Pattison, Managing Director, The Jim Pattison Group

Perhaps the most telling detail about Jim Pattison is that he wears a watch on each arm. One is a double watch that provides Eastern Standard and European time; the other gives him the time in his native Vancouver. The watches are the sign of a practical man who has his mind on the global picture—who regards international time zones as inconveniences to be surmounted.

He must be on to something. As sole owner of the Jim Pattison Group, a vast international conglomerate, his is the forty-fifth largest company in Canada and the fourth largest that is privately held. His sales will have reached nearly $3 billion in 1992, his assets are more than $1 billion, and he boasts 13,000 employees.

"We take the basic position that there is no border," he says of his business philosophy. "We get up in the morning and say: 'Can we compete with the guys in Seattle? Or the guys in Texas or Buffalo or California or New York?' Our whole attitude is that we've got to take on the Americans in every single business we're in—in terms of quality, service and competitive pricing. If we can't, we either fix the business, shut it down or sell it."

His straight shooting is also typical of the kind of self-made man who didn't bother to graduate from university—he was nine credits short of a degree when he left the University of British Columbia. "I got caught up in a business deal and never finished," he says with characteristic understatement. "I always intended to go back but I never did."

What stopped him was a budding career in the car business. To make ends meet at college, he worked washing cars at a used-car lot—and managed to sell several cars to his fellow students. Armed with his confidence as a salesman, he put his house and life insurance on the line to get a loan from the Royal Bank to buy his own car dealership. That was in 1961. By 1967 he had the largest auto dealership in western Canada.

Today, his enterprises span a wide variety of industries in five different market areas: transportation, communications, food products, packaging and financial services. He owns grocery stores, pharmacies, fish operations, sign companies, magazine and book distributorships, automobile dealerships and radio stations, among other things. One of his oddest business ventures: he owns twenty-two Ripley's Believe It Or Not museums around the world.

The range is indicative of the renaissance businessman he is— he sees nothing random about the diversity he has managed so well. "You sell cars, you sell to a customer," he says, with his trademark directness. "You sell packaging or books, you're selling products to consumers. We've always had a kind of thread that tends to be toward the consumer side of things."

But despite the gambles he's always been prepared to take, he ran up against a conservative banking environment when he started out. "In the early days, getting support from Canadian banks was my biggest problem," he says. "I finally had to go to Wall Street and my initial support came from the Americans. As time went by, the banks—particularly the Toronto-Dominion—made an enormous positive contribution to our company. We wouldn't be where we are today if the TD hadn't stepped in in the early seventies and backed us solidly."

Legend has it that Pattison is not above theatrics to get his staff solidly behind him, too; the story goes that he once tossed a rock through a window to get attention from his employees at a meeting. But he justifies such actions as stemming from a deep sense of responsibility to those who work for him. "We think a company that doesn't make money can't offer any security to its employees and families," he says. "The only security is working for a healthy company. If you're losing cash or market share, everyone ends up in trouble."

And as far as he's concerned, the same reasoning extends to the business environment in Canada today. "If we're going to keep the standard of living we've got in this country, we've got to have major productivity gains," he argues. "We need them in labor and we need them in management. I don't think Canadian management works nearly as hard, is nearly as innovative or hustles nearly as much as our American counterparts. Competitiveness is about prosperity—my prosperity and your prosperity. If we don't have productivity, it's going to affect our standard of living. It'll mean we'll have less to put into mortgage payments, car payments—everything. That's what competitiveness is about."

If Pattison sounds opinionated, he says he comes by his opinions honestly. "I've made every kind of mistake you can think of," he admits of his years in business. "When articles in *Fortune* magazine or *Business Week* or the *Globe and Mail* talk about what went wrong for a particular business, all my mistakes are there. I've bought at the wrong time, mismanaged things at times, made a lot of mistakes in people I've chosen. But fortunately I've been able to hang in there during the down periods, and our better decisions up until now have outweighed our bad ones. I think I make fewer mistakes today because as you get older you tend to become more conservative—you take less risks."

Still, Pattison is nothing if not a risk taker. And he echoes the common themes of other risk takers about what is preventing Canada from achieving international competitiveness: overregulation on the part of government, too many levels of management, and punitive labor costs. "In 1980, our production costs were two percent higher than the Americans," he points out. "Now they're forty percent higher. We can't make it this way. We've got to get down to reality." His ventures serve as a model of that reality, although he says he had no idea at the start of his career that he'd be heading up such a large, eclectic empire.

"In my wildest imaginings, I never dreamed all this would happen," he says of his accomplishments. "But I really work at making a go of things and I find it's not as hard as you'd think to keep a handle on the different concerns. Over the years, I've learned how to keep fairly good controls in key areas. The businesses are like kids. As you grow them up, you get to know them pretty well. You know what their strengths and weaknesses are—and who the people are that you can count on."

He also shares another common characteristic with those succeeding in Canada today: he loves what he does.

"It's fun going to work in the morning," says Pattison, who is notorious for putting in long hours at his Vancouver headquarters. "I haven't found anything that's more fun than business up until now."

Susan Murray, President, S.A. Murray Consulting Inc.

Conventional wisdom has it that lobbyists are smarmy gladhanders who sidle up to government power brokers with narrow agendas dictated by their business clients. Wrong economy, says new-style lobbyist Susan Murray. In a global business environment, with Canada struggling to find its footing, there's no room for short-term deals between business and government carved out at someone's expense. The new lobbyist is a shuttle diplomat who works the two sectors to everyone's benefit with an eye on the long term.

Murray not only epitomizes the genre, she may well have invented it. As president and founder of S.A. Murray Consulting, she runs a twenty-five person lobbying operation that will have billed about $3.5 million in 1992. Her client list has included such players as Massey-Ferguson, Hughes Aircraft and the Ontario auto-insurance sector.

"I saw a market niche that had been totally untapped," she says of the business she founded in 1982 armed with an honors degree in political science and experience as a strategist and vice president for the Ontario Tories. "It seemed to me that government and business really didn't know how to talk to each other—that each sector had a lot of knee-jerk responses to the other. And that was preventing us from solving regulatory and other issues that were keeping us from becoming competitive. Canada was falling behind."

Murray's niche in the new economy is one that is in fact helping drive the new economy forward. She's an agent for change—and a beneficiary of that change, as well. She has all the trademarks of successful Canadian entrepreneurship as we move toward the millennium. But she still sees logjams along the way.

"As the economy restructures, my business grows exponentially," she says. "More and more companies are reducing the layers of management. They're becoming competitive and we can help them with their government relations. But what we really need now is change in the way government works. That same flattening out of traditional hierarchies hasn't hit the government yet. There are still a lot of layers to contend with. In fact, the problem is we've got a nineteenth century structure of government at the same time that we're trying to get our companies to work within a twenty-first century world. No wonder the two have been colliding."

Increasingly, hers is the company other firms come to if they want legislation changed or laws written to help them. Like a good union arbitrator, she moves comfortably back and forth between the two camps until she brings each around to the other's viewpoint.

"Susan is one of those courageous people who can enter a man's world," says her friend Marti Smye, president of People Tech, a human resources consulting firm. "The stereotype of lobbyists is one of guys who smoke cigars and make deals in the back room. But Susan's handled things in a straightforward, up-front fashion. I think she'd done a marvelous job."

Using information as her primary tool, Murray has recently won a number of battles for her clients. Among them: working for the CEO of The Bay and three other client companies, she won an amendment to Ontario law to permit stores to open on Sunday. "Sunday shopping had been an issue for fifteen years when we got involved," she says. "But in six months we managed to get the government to reverse its position and allow for wide-open Sunday shopping."

If she's an insider with some influence among the powers-that-be, she got there by doing her homework. "When the government approved Sunday opening just for the holiday season, we tracked the impact on sales tax, sales and jobs. We also did a shopping basket comparison of Becker's and Mac's Milk, who were against Sunday shopping, and proved they charge ten to twenty percent more for each item. As usual, the consumer was suffering, too. In other words, we compiled all the economic data. That way we could go to the government and say: 'Not opening on Sundays is having a real effect on our retailers' ability to survive.' And we could support our case with figures."

Although Murray's company is now one of the leading government- relations consulting firms in the country, it wasn't always thus.

"There's no question it was really hard in the first few years," she admits. "We didn't operate in the old-boy network style of schmoozing and lunching and paying political donations. It was hard to convince business at the beginning that there was a better way—and to convince government that we weren't just another group of opportunists. I lost a lot of contracts early on because people would say I didn't have the glitter at the political level because I never hired politicians or ex-Cabinet ministers. I just hired people who rolled up their sleeves."

Many of the traditional lobbying firms, she says, didn't take her seriously as a result. Their shortsightedness has helped her dominate her field in Ontario. "There are competitors of ours who'll use political contacts or government information without contributing anything back," she says. "We always go to government with solutions because government is so big and has so many crisis issues. We go in and say: 'why don't you look at the following options and let's see if we can work from there?' We cooperate. We never scream and yell, which used to be the traditional style of lobbying."

She says that critical to her work is her ability to build trust between the corporate world and the various governments, and she cites her cooly rational approach as one of her strongest assets. She cuts through the emotional arguments on both sides to zero in on the real issues. The process can be long and grueling, but it usually works. A case in point was when the NDP government in Ontario was leaning toward nationalizing auto insurance. Murray and her team were instrumental in the decision to dump the plan. "We explained to the government that they didn't have to own the industry to regulate it—they could still protect the consumer," she says. "Again, we did economic models showing the cost of buying the industry, the spin-off jobs that would be lost, the impact on suppliers, tax-based and industry head offices that would be affected. They were complex models. We said, 'Why should the taxpayer be asked to buy an industry?' It was going to cost billions. We said to the government, 'If it's just ideology, there are better ways than nationalizing the industry.' It took us a year, but they listened."

Now she has her sights set on a massive regulatory reform project within the agricultural chemical industry in a bid to give Canadian farmers a fighting chance. "Our farmers were becoming less competitive because environmental concerns were blocking the way for new pesticides and herbicides to be registered here," she explains. "In fact the new science makes these products less harmful. So we brought together the key players—the farmers, environmentalists, consumers and the chemical industry—and organized a task force to solve the issues. That's the new lobbying model. Pulling everyone together instead of fighting. We're educating all the people responsible for making decisions."

Yves Guérard, Chairman and CEO, Sobeco, Ernst and Young Inc.

Yves Guérard has assessed the risk of Canada's failing to adapt to a new economic environment—and pronounced it too high. He should know. As an actuary, his profession entails calculating risks and premiums for the insurance industry. But he's also always been adept at seeing beyond the rows of figures and sheets of tables endemic to his field. Growing up during

World War II in the small Quebec town of St-Félix de Valois, Guérard remembers his father hanging a map of Europe in his general store, replete with flags and thumbtacks tracking the Allied and Axis armies. As the ten-year-old Guérard stocked shelves or delivered orders, the neighbors would congregate to discuss the latest events in Europe. Guérard, now chairman and CEO of the management consulting firm Sobeco, Ernst and Young, credits that early exposure to international politics with helping shape his global view today. "It was like having a window on the world," he says, "It was the initial seed that got me started looking outward."

The actuarial profession hasn't traditionally been a hotbed of forward thinking, so Guérard's broad vision is particularly remarkable given the milieu in which he operates. But his ability to grasp the big issues is what characterizes him—and what makes him a player in helping shape the new economy.

Today, actuarial work accounts for only one third of his firm's business. Human-resources services and computer-systems development are responsible for the remaining two-thirds.

"I think we're living through a very important transition and that we'll recognize it in retrospect," he emphasizes. "We have to be multidisciplinary now, because our world's becoming both multidisciplinary and multinational. When our clients come to us with a problem, they don't want to be told that actually they have fourteen problems and will need fourteen specialists to solve them. They want us to take a global perspective and come back with responses that will cover all their concerns. We are in the solution business, after all, and we have to adapt our ways."

He says what that means is that his firm has to have its finger on the pulse of the most advanced business practices throughout the world. "Many of our clients have operations that cross national barriers," he points out. "So having a window on the outside is really important. We have to be able to access and use information from everywhere. We need to know what solutions other people came up with in Peru or Belgium, and how they can be adapted here."

But while he's something of a renaissance thinker—he likes to keep abreast of the latest scientific theories about the Big Bang—his trademark is his ability to turn theory into nuts-and-bolts practice for his clientele. As he puts it: "We're not publishing master's theses or PhDs. We're serving clients. In the practical world, what clients need is to solve their problems for the foreseeable future, to not compromise their position and to have some room to maneuver. They don't want you necessarily to go on an intellectual trip every time they have a problem. You have to put yourself in their shoes to find out what they really need."

Typical of the kind of service and product his firm is involved in is a multifunctional library software package, which is now being successfully marketed around the world. A totally integrated system, it does everything including opening the library lights in the morning and shutting them off at night. It looks after purchasing, inventory, research, the lending of books, statistics, budget control—every aspect of library management. And Guérard is well aware of the impact such programs can have on personnel.

"There's tremendous pressure in industry to reduce the number of tiers of management," he stresses. "Large companies in the past sometimes had a span of ten levels between the president and the worker. In the future, they're going to have to make do with five or even fewer levels. With a PC on the desk, a president can now access information that would have taken two weeks to get before through the chain of command. Obviously, when you can shorten that chain, you can cut costs and accelerate the reaction time. And you also enrich the job of the people who are at the end of the line."

He believes people and business must constantly evolve to meet new economic challenges in an ever-developing world order. But it frustrates him that so many companies are taking so long to make the changes necessary for survival from now on into the next century. He cites the reluctance to face change as one of the major barriers preventing Canada from moving forward.

"It's an attitude thing," he muses. "People aren't comfortable with change—and that's what has to be overcome. Actually, more than just accepting change, you've got to seek it. You have to abandon the comfort of a well-established position and go conquer a new one. Not doing so is probably the biggest hurdle Canada has to overcome. It's like the old saying, you know: 'We met the enemy—and it was us!' "

In keeping with that philosophy, Guérard expects his company to evolve over the next five years into something radically different from what it is today. "A lot more different than we think," he stresses. "In the area of human resources in particular, I suspect we're going to be driven by all the changes taking place in the market. The restructuring of industry and services is going to be accompanied by a restructuring of the way work is spread out."

He predicts the work-at-home revolution will finally take off. "I don't think it's a dream any more," he says. "I can see many more people working outside the office on computer networks or some other form of link—and from an environmental viewpoint that makes sense. Think of the decrease in the number of cars generating carbon monoxide."

For Guérard, change and risk are at the heart of the entrepreneurship that will see Canada become competitive. He believes Canada is in full development, and that much of that development involves the creation of new technologies, systems and software, as well as more extensive training of personnel.

"Some cultures value risk, individual initiative, innovation and independence," he said in a 1989 speech. "Others channel entrepreneurial currents toward the social, cultural and nonprofit sectors. ... Canada will be more entrepreneurial if each city, community and region becomes entrepreneurial. National policies can help—or at least not create barriers—but it will be the combined action of many entrepreneurs throughout the country that will make Canada more entrepreneurial. An entrepreneur is not a dreamer or a speculator, but someone who takes a calculated risk. Not a gambler, but rather someone who studies a company's conditions for success and eliminates unnecessary risks. But mainly, entrepreneurship is based on the ability to make the jump—to leave the comfortable status quo and follow the belief in a good idea. This will and determination are important resources for a community that wants to prosper. And we've got to develop those attitudes in each of our citizens."

Robert Flynn, President and CEO, Nutrasweet

"What you need to succeed in global business is the ability to see opportunities around the world. You need to be able to transcend your nationality, and you don't shrink if you find that your primary market is not next door... In fact, you're turned on by the fact that it's not next door." That's Bob Flynn, Canadian-born, Canadian still, but president and CEO of a billion-dollar global company that has developed some strikingly successful products, and marketed them brilliantly, chief among them Aspartame—Nutrasweet of "look for the swirl" fame.

Flynn wasn't talking about himself (although he could have been). He was talking about one of his employees, Brazilian-born Paulino Barros, and of the process of developing a blockbuster product. "Paulino is totally product-oriented. He works for Nutrasweet. Nutrasweet has supurb technologies. Paulino thinks, 'What products do people like to eat?' He thinks—eggs. But the yolks of eggs are loaded with fat and cholesterol, and doctors everywhere are telling men, 'Don't eat eggs, eggs are sure killers for men.'"

Flynn, whose role in this story is to be the final yes-or-no decision-maker, continues: "So Paulino asks, 'How can we extract the fat and cholesterol from eggs without altering their taste, and without getting regulatory approval?' That's really important, because if you need to get regulatory approval, it'll be five to eight years before you get a regulator's blessing."

"Paulino then figures out how to do it, using the same technique used to get instant coffee—a super-critical fluid extraction process. But there's bad news: it's too costly. And there's an environmental challenge—what do you do with all the stuff you extract? We can't just dump it somewhere."

"So Paulino then looks around the world for who uses fat and cholesterol. And he finds a growing market: the cosmetics industry and shrimp farming. So he asks them, 'How much do you want, and how much will you pay?' Now he gets down to business, forms a partnership with a group of technical people in Germany, SKW, and his team perfects a mechanical process that takes an egg and gives you back an egg with ninty-six percent of the fat removed and a hundred percent of the cholesterol removed. A *mechanical* process—no regulatory approval required, because the egg is still an egg. It's not an egg *product*— people don't like buying egg *products,* or bread *products,* they like buying eggs and bread. So what we have here is fat-free, cholesterol-free eggs that are going to be a blockbuster for us."

But the story isn't over yet. You can see the making of the plan, and the process that goes into the making of the product. Now comes the marketing. Flynn says they aren't particularly interested in marketing directly to the consumer, so they look at where most eggs are consumed. "As it turns out, the baking industry uses more eggs than anyone. And they're really happy to have this product. The other thing Paulino did was that he went to the dairy industry and said to them, 'You guys have seen an enormous decline in your ability to sell eggs, since doctors are down on them. Well, we have a process that'll help you sell more eggs, because eggs still are eggs. So the dairy industry is onside instead of being worried we had a substitute product that would undercut their business. What's Paulino got? Well, he was a Brazilian at birth, but he sees globally. He works directly for a guy named Joe Maloney, who was the executive director for United Way, but has such fantasic managerial capability that we got him to come here. And what we all have is this ability to apply whatever skills we have to global markets."

From Flynn's point of view, this latter perspective is particularly important. "Most companies," he says, "look outward and ask themselves, 'What does the world need?' and then set out to supply it even if they don't have the skills. That approach is fraught with danger. What we do here is ask ourselves, 'What do we do exceptionally well? Who could use our skills?' Much smarter."

But what is it, we wanted to know, that sets him and his colleagues apart, that gives them the ability to see what's possible and then follow through and make it happen? "I put it down to two things in myself," says Flynn. "First, I was born in Canada. My mother was French, my father Irish-Scots. I was brought up understanding that you have to be sensitive to the other guys, we weren't all the same. And I got a Canadian education. Much as Canadians bitch about the education system, it's like night and day from the education Americans get. Second, I got the best piece of advice a young man could ever get. I was thirty-two , and had just been made general manager of Carborundum. It was their tradition that the new general manager have lunch with the board. So I went for lunch, and Bill McCormack was on that board. He took me aside and said, 'Listen, Bob, we're given only a small time on earth, so don't get your priorities screwed up. You'll fade to obscurity if day after day the process of accumulating wealth or power isn't fun. So no matter how big your title, if it isn't fun, get out.' So I've lived by that. When a young fellow comes to me with an idea, I'll let him spend a bit of the company's time and money. What you have to understand is that you don't risk the whole firm, but there's a lot of fun in taking a chance."

Thirteen

Are We There Yet, Daddy?

*If the Creator had a purpose in equipping us with a
neck, he certainly meant for us to stick it out.*
                                        —*Arthur Koestler*

THE WORST THING that could happen to Canada is that we
maintain the status quo. That single fact would ensure a steady
decline, not just in our overall standard and quality of life,
but in the opportunities we might have to take part in the bur-
geoning global economy.

The danger is that Canada could become a dinosaur among
nations. Known principally for our vast and timeless spaces,
we now find that the new world economy has eclipsed time
and space. Organized as an industrial economy, we find that
the world has moved on to an information economy. Canada
is a great trading nation, to be sure, but one whose trade is
almost exclusively linked to business cycles—while the business cycle's been superseded by the product cycle.

These worldwide changes affect more than Canada. The
information revolution—characterized by consumer television, Hollywood films and fax machines—has wiped out the
Soviet Empire and brought almost a quarter of Europe's population back into a market economy—except that today's
market economy is strikingly different from those of other

eras. A great many power shifts have occurred. And these have not been kind to Canada—at least on the surface of things. Countries used to have sovereignty over their interest rates. Now interest rates are set by international investors and business people. And capital is a worldwide phenomenon. Canada hopes for economic growth. But economic growth no longer stimulates employment or output as much as it once did. In short, you don't need the things we do well to get rich. And if we continue to do these things in the way we've "always done them," we'll be worse off—because that's how the market works. Unfortunately, despite the clear emergence of successful information-based business in Canada, the signs in 1992 are that too many Canadians are continuing their sleepwalk into economic decline. Our biggest trouble is that Canada is still not internationally competitive in the new sectors the way it is in its natural resource sectors.

Knowledge-based industries are soaking up the labor force, creating thousands of jobs. There are, for example, 150,000 software developers in Canada alone, a job that didn't exist twenty years ago, about the same as are directly employed in the pulp and paper industry Canada-wide. Sales of computer services and software in Canada top $4 billion a year. Hardware? Well, Canada doesn't make a lot of PCs—but we do make telecom switches, which aren't that different. Domestic market sales are around $5 billion, and Canada has a positive trade balance in switches, but it's tiny: $205 million.

Canada's pulp and paper industry sells more than $14 billion, of which more than eighty-five percent, $12 billion, is generated by exports.

So the problem is that our knowledge-based sectors are not yet generating the massive sales or the huge positive trade balance our resource sector generates. We're moving more and more people into the sector, and it can sustain itself internationally. But it's not yet ready to support the country as a whole. It's difficult to know for sure, but it looks as if the world's moving away from dependence on natural resources faster than Canada is.

There's no sign the public sector is willing to stop spending and return the country to the black. There's no way the transitions can be made properly when government-administered prices and taxes continue to rise while other prices continue to fall. It's paradoxical but true that every transitional growth engine—from railways to cars to computers—has been characterized by falling—not rising—real prices as their economic dominance increased. Companies that have moved quickly into the new economy will simply transfer their important operations out of Canada to avoid the tax-price whipsaw. The loss will be Canada's. Already we see this occurring in such vital growth areas as corporate telecommunications centers. Loss of that major client market will likely consign Canada to telecommunications backwater status, even if our cities are all digitally wired by the end of the nineties.

Unfortunately for Canada, our elites have not served us well. Our politicians have believed too long in politics as usual. There are two aspects to this. First, as in most other western countries—but more so in proportion to our GDP— our politicians continue to bribe the voters with our own money, using the rhetoric of the pursuit of social justice while tearing down our ability to make economic adjustments. Second, and distinctly Canadian, we've allowed them to stoke the flames of the family quarrel rather than getting down to the business of putting our economic house in order.

Our business elites have done no better. Rather than championing the waves of change, they've embraced free trade without understanding its implications. They've continued to believe that resources and a falling dollar would save the day.

What If We Did Everything Right?

What would it look like? Well, for one thing, we'd live in smart houses, and we'd have smart TVs, smart computers, smart phones. All these gadgets, which are now a pain to use, would be a pleasure. They'd anticipate our moods and routinely give us what we want. Remember wives? It would almost be like having a wife (yes, lots of women professionals would also like someone to have the house ready when they return exhausted after trying to soar like an eagle in the company of the turkeys around the office.) If you like dining before eight, the meal would be approaching serving readiness as you came in the door. The house colors would shift to suit your mood. The music/news/entertainment/data you prefer would be ready for your consultation. You get the picture.

Kids? Well, even now, their sitter of choice is the TV. But in the new world, you'd have the control. Plus the school could come right into the home. The classroom could be of world dimensions, and information would be provided from world-class providers wherever they happened to be.

Maybe the most exciting development of all would be the impact on the manufacturing and service side. The argument's already been made that manufacturing and services can no longer be meaningfully distinguished. The information highway would blur this distinction even further because it would enable the shift to so-called "agile manufacturing." Remember the sushi bar model: a few general-purpose modules that can be combined in many ways with added sauces and other ingredients to produce a customized dish in seconds. Ditto for products: you want a family size van that handles like a sports car and is as sleek and upscale as a Jag? Take one of these, a couple of those and one of these... Orders, plans, controls whiz around the continental production network positioning the components along with millions of other custom orders, the production path is optimized and in 24 hours later or less you can pick up your personalized transportation system, as individualized as you and technology can make it.

Lehigh Unversity's Iacocca Institute put together a futures report with the help of a number of industry executives. The sweeping report posits a future in which agile manufacturers dominate the industrial world. Unlike the mass producers of today, agile manufacturers will build to order highly customized, reconfigurable products—an individualized car that can be upgraded later if the driver wants to add bells and whistles; a small batch of specialized semiconductors priced the same as larger lots; or a computing-communications machine programmed to a user's specs and shipped twenty-four hours after it is ordered. Texas Instruments' John Patterson, quoted in *Electronics Magazine*, a respected industry publication, says, "The dawn of agile manufacturing represents a unique opportunity for the United States to reclaim industrial dominance—probably the last opportunity we're going to have." Such service will be possible thanks to highly flexible robotic assembly lines that can be swiftly reprogrammed for new tasks. To speed production and aid cooperation, factories will be linked by a broadband communications clearinghouse, the Factory Americas Network, which will enable them to locate suppliers and designers, and to share information, all at a keystroke.

The network will also facilitate the rapid formation of "virtual companies"—joint ventures among multiple corporate units working cooperatively to seize a market opportunity. Management will be decentralized—"self-managed work teams" will be the rule, not the exception, says Patterson—and information will flow freely among R&D, shop floor and boardroom.

Sound too off-the-wall? The only thing holding this stuff back in Canada is an outmoded regulatory and social structure. When Jacques Cartier and his crew dumped writing, books and navigational information on the first inhabitants of North America, they hadn't much use for them. Their societies weren't organized in ways that gave value to those items. But the items themselves, and the technology they represented, were state-of-the-art for their day. North America now belongs to their descendants (although we're having second thoughts and transferring it back). We face a similar situation with today's state-of-the-art transforming technology. Except that socially we're not ready to make better use of it. The consequences haven't changed in five hundred years: catch up or lose out.

The challenge is clear—how to take a resource-based, industrially organized economy and transform it into something more closely approximating an economy for the global, information age.

It is happening. The hardships of slow growth *are* changing Canada's financial management culture—ever so slowly—to bring it closer to entrepreneurship, to breed a new group of intermediaries combining top management skills and credibility in capital markets. Then, too, the prospect of low inflation promises a return to normal yield curves (with higher rewards for "patient" capital) and greater returns to innovators than to speculators.

In other sectors, too, change is powering forward: engineering schools and business schools are seeking international partnerships with specific industries and even companies. Their graduates are generally highly trained bilingual, or multilingual ambitious professionals. They have the skills, knowledge and competitive attitude required to create and manage first-class production and distribution platforms that master the product cycle.

But what more is there to say to provide guidance to those who are trying to promote change in Canada? There's this for sure:

- Governments are broke. Don't even think of using government money. It'll be hard enough to hang on to your own during the start-up phases.
- Elites have no vision and less cash. They won't understand what you're trying to do. More important, they're

out of speculation money, too. They probably have too many 1980s businesses that are going sour in the 1990s, such as property development, banking and owning the aircraft that fly people around the country. Anything left over, they're keeping for their kids.

- Your market has to be ordinary people, most of whom are forty-something and struggling. No big cash. But if you can save this market money, time, headaches or even one of the above, they'll pay you something.
- That big market is really umpteen niche markets with the major determining factor in the buy/don't buy decision not the income of the buyer, but the life-style. Everyone talks on the phone. But not for the same reason. So they won't relate to a new phone service the same way. You'll have to dig out their reason if you want to make a sale. They all watch TV—but not the same things, and most in ways that avoid advertising. Lots are couch potatoes. Lots still coach Little League baseball and soccer. In other words, we've seen the end of mass marketing—the niches are getting smaller and the consumer more demanding. Says marketing guru Faith Popcorn, "What will make us buy one product over another is a feeling of partnership with the seller, and a feeling we're buying for the future. Anonymous, impersonal selling is over."
- To win, you have to introduce the product in as many markets as possible around the world, and then use your market share to add value to your product. Says Popcorn, "Interactive warranties for things like appliances, entertainment units, home-office equipment will soon be faxed from the point of purchase to the manufacturer. Corporate reps will get in touch with consumers to find out if they're happy—within days of purchase."

A Major Canadian Turnaround Project

Let your mind wander through the options that build on our existing strengths, and could trampoline the whole country into the new economy. Here's one possibility: a voice, data, video, electronic superhighway. Remember way back near the beginning of this book the transportation analogy—a transportation network was the spine that moved people and product to where they were needed to succeed brilliantly in the transition to an industrial economy. Similarly in the information economy, a communications network with lots of highways to move information to where it's needed: a fast highway to send feature films across in seconds, a less exotic one to send this book along in minutes.

If Canada had this highway, we'd be up to speed and maybe a little ahead of the United States and maybe five to ten years ahead of anywhere else in the world. Think of all the information that floats around, from stock market quotes to research papers. All that stuff moves electronically now. But it's time-consuming and somewhat difficult—too many different commands. So a lot of important connections don't get made.

This difficulty shows up in surprising ways. For instance, while it's much easier to start a company in North America than anywhere else in the world, it's still time-consuming and expensive to file papers. The potential electronic highway could change that because every government office would be linked to it, and the technology would include the transmission of signatures, video telephoning, and so on.

The same advantages could occur for paying taxes and handling all sorts of interfaces with large bureaucracies. How? Like a VCR, these networks would permit time shifting. And the technology would be sufficiently advanced that you'd have your choice of medium —telephone (voice), handwriting (notepad) or typewritten inputs. Other advantages are also obvious: video conferencing, exchange of documents without having to create paper copies first, including check clearing, research papers, information of all kinds.

Plus, because this "electronic highway" would be publicly accessible, the things would become an enormous bazaar, a carnival of chat, services, arcana and so on, a kind of medieval fair of variety of every description—some shocking, some valuable, most just pleasurable interchanges among like-minded people.

What's more, this highway would provide the backbone for giving Canada a leading role in agile manufacturing, smart housing and the other stuff mentioned at the top of the chapter. Building this kind of highway would be getting us closer to being there—late, but there nevertheless.

Both Canada and the United States have already established the elements of this network, although it primarily handles computer electronic mail, bulletin boards and exchanges between university profs. Europe's not far behind. This highway would raise the potential of interchanges by several orders of magnitude. And it would include multimedia capabilities that would immensely enrich our lives.

Since everyone will benefit from this enhancement, why don't we have it? The answer brings us back to our institutional drag and concomitant vested interests. Our regulators, who reflect the public will, are vainly struggling to keep separate the technologies that this highway would bring together. They're selling licenses whose meaning would be eradicated if this network went public. If anyone can unload a video, who needs a cable monopoly? What about Canadian content? What about provincial jurisdictions over education? What about certifying professional qualifications? Let's face it, a highway like this would drastically alter everything. For the better. At one end of the highway would be the consumer and at the other end the service provider. The beneficiaries of the present system—broadcasters, cable companies, telephone companies and resellers— would be out of the system and would have to find a different role to play.

How To Finance the Highway?

Here are four private-sector possibilities.

- Just build the network and open it up to service providers at affordable rates—probably the same as now. The hope here is that the overwhelming public acclaim would force a giant reorganization of the economy, especially the financial, manufacturing and research communities.

- Build the network for particular publics before joining them all at once—a kind of niche-market-financed "pre-build." Again, go for ability to pay. University or research-center networks would be cheaper than some corporate networks. This approach would retain most of the previous alternative's advantages with the added advantage of lower financing costs, because the revenues from one group of users could be used to finance expansion.

- Combine fiber and cable networks and start to offer services into the home over existing structures as part of a cable contract or phone service. This strategy would crunch today's barriers and ask the regulators to play catch-up. A powerful case could be made that the regulators have violated any social contract by putting the nation's future at risk through their dilatory behavior.

- Forget land-based systems and use satellites. Work on miniaturizing equipment that will make the network interactive. This alternative may in fact take place while the debate continues over the land-based approach. The only drawback to satellites is the quality of the transmission. As a bypass technique, this technology is already richly used.

Once the systems are in place, the users of the systems would become the main public supporters of the systems. The network would link all elements of the multi-media mix. But individual elements could continue to be supplied by separate elements. The result is competition between different delivery modes. But some regulation would be necessary at the end of the day to keep prices from following each other upward. The name of the regulatory formula: a rate cap. But within the cap the only rule should be "anything goes."

While all this is occurring, parallel technologies would also be at work—especially radio and cellular. Yes, your computer modem could work by radio or cellular to bypass the network and access distant data sources using radio links to local phone networks. These would act as additional disciplinarians on the network price.

What's It All About, Alfie?

If you haven't put the book down and lost your place yet, you know that the argument here is that Canada's a relatively low-growth, high-cost, industrially organized country undergoing a painful transition to a new economy—an information-based, global economy—that could once again establish itself as a world leading economy. All we have to do to get there is make it through the transition period. How will we do that? How are we going to finance the transitions we have to make as a country? Well, you've met some of the new entrepreneurs with the products and the new forms of company to deal with corporate financing problems in this kind of climate. One such new boy on the block is Stormont Investments, formed by two high-tech entrepreneurs—Rod Bryden, founder of Systemhouse, and Hugh McDiarmid, former CEO of Lumonics, both Ottawa-based high-tech companies that established worldwide reputations and significant market shares.

Helping CEOs to manage corporate transition stages is Stormont's mission. Its business is to work with the owner or the board of directors or the chief executive officer, the very top of business, typically mid-sized business, to assist "first in defining their objective of success—what success is in a definable time frame—and then to define with the principals a strategy to achieve it, and then to manage its actual achievement," says Rod Bryden.

We need these new intermediaries, because many of the old ones aren't doing what they used to do. Real estate losses, for example, haven't yet been accounted for by financial institutions in North America. We're witnessing no-bid markets now, and real estate price declines from the top of the market are getting closer to fifty percent than thirty percent. Those losses to both borrowers and lenders haven't been registered, so lending institutions aren't going to be as accommodating as they used to be. Says Bill Mackness, at the University of Manitoba, "This won't stop everything dead in its tracks, but it's not what a real snappy growth picture's made of. These institutions have been burned bad... They're looking at fifteen percent and twenty percent vacancy rates in principal properties in all the major cities, not enough cash flow to cover debt obligations on fully leveraged properties, and the rents are coming down."

The key to financing a company in this kind of climate is convincing your would-be investor that the company has outstanding management. "Every corporation is responsible as a corporate entity to get the best return on the assets they have, whatever they make. It's the ability of management to do that," says Vancouver's pension fund manager Milton Wong. This new requirement for management to stand out is the result of a shift from the 1970s, where gains from inflation were a certainty, to today's ground-floor price climate where rewards instead go to innovators and achievers and are far from automatically passed around.

Today's world is no longer homogeneous. For example, say the price of lumber's gone up. That doesn't mean every lumber company's going to make money. Management skills, their strategies and their commitment to the shareholders make the difference. Wong says, "In too many of the mature companies, managers of the assets aren't compensated to be really passionate about their work. But in a general sense, if management wants to win and be the best in the world, it can happen."

For an investment manager who focuses on quality, finding "beautiful companies" isn't hard. Wong says, "Look at the quality and the management, at whether they've got major share ownership, at whether they have management skills from previous work. You look at the margin in business, and you want it to be two times more than it might be in a competing company. Northwest Company is an example, says Wong. Eddie Bauer is another. "There are a whole host of companies like that—the winners are emerging and they generally seem to be smaller companies."

That's who's really growing—them and people who have taken a global approach. The Corels with Corel Draw!, Powerhouse and the Boston linkage that they have created, Newbridge Gandalf, who've had a tough time, but they've recognized the need to broaden the horizon and move into the international sphere. It's a hard lesson, but we have to go outside Canada in a lot of our businesses. Mark Potter at Cognos tried to succeed from a Canadian marketing platform and couldn't do it. So he brought in the marketing muscle, set it up in Boston and said, "Run the marketing business out of Boston... We'll develop products and technology here in Ottawa but you guys do the marketing," And that's been a tremendous breakthrough.

This new investment climate can shake up the big boys, too. In the larger companies, the shareholders and boards are demanding that management restructure to meet the new competitive areas. A number of companies have done reasonably well. In the mass transit market Bombardier is moving well on a global competitive basis. Stelco's moving now, with their back against the wall: new management's assessing its assets and where it can compete effectively.

Another lever at work is the way pension funds have changed. A lot of legislation and controversy over pension money has moved the growth of the country's pension savings from defined benefit plans to defined contribution plans, that is, the RRSP market. The banks are front and center in these funds. And people are much more educated investors today. The information flow, in terms of accessible publications and seminars, is fantastic. Then there's the slump in Japan, up to now the world's biggest foreign investor. That, too, will intensify competition for investment. The decline in Japan's market is bigger than that of 1929 in the United States. From 1989 to now, the Nikkei average has moved from more than forty thousand down to sixteen thousand. The balloon has burst there.

But on some home fronts, the lesson is: home-grow your own top talent. That's what they're doing on the west coast. The investment community is supporting a two-year portfolio management course at UBC. Eighty students manage as much as $800,000, getting hands-on experience trading securities under the tutelage of more than a hundred volunteers from the business. Milton Wong's happy with them. He set up the course, and he's confident these youngsters will know the right stuff.

Overcoming complex transaction management is where companies like Stormont step in. Hugh McDiarmid says, "Our client's the CEO. He may understand his business but not have an operational understanding of how financing and the capital markets work. Or alternatively the CEO will be a deal maker and a capital market specialist and a financial restructurer, like my partner Rod (Bryden) was with Systemhouse, and not necessarily be a full-time day-to-day involved-in-the-business kind of guy. We're offering those CEOs the opportunity to do what they do best. Stormont can do the other stuff and create value."

Is leadership a factor? Certainly. And here again, there are hopeful signs. It just may be that the climate for leadership is gradually changing for the better. People are taking the lead. They're turning off and tuning out the elitist solutions ("let us qualified people make the decisions") in favor of the populism ("ordinary people are well able to decide how they want to live their lives") the information economy lets flourish. "Inadequate leadership is unlikely to be tolerated much longer," says Rod Bryden. "People are beginning to value leadership because they see the consequences of not having it." And, in an information economy, leaders will have to have not just a vision, but the ability to cultivate a listening culture. "The old command-and-control style of leadership won't work in a complex environment that changes rapidly, communicates instantly and relies on a diverse work force for results," says Heublein marketing vice president Martin Pazzani. Effective leaders are the ones who listen—to their customers, their employees, their constituents—and then empower them. Matching these changes are changes in Canada's business incentive structure to displace custodians of other people's money and begin to reward entrepreneurs—not just because of declining inflation, but also because the world of professionals is losing its clubby charm and becoming more cutthroat every day.

Put it all together and there are signs the country can get through this time of trial. But the Canada that emerges will be very different from Canada 1992. It will have an attractive investment climate, a coherent approach to regulation that works with markets instead of against them. It will encourage information flows and entrepreneurship. It will even have public spending under control, with social programs funded according to sound economic principles and taken out of the political arena. It will have an education system that puts the best teachers and the best sources of knowledge into every home that wants them. In mastering the process of change, Canadians will have rediscovered some constant truths: that the best guarantee of a sound and progressive collectivity is to favor individual achievement; and that countries exist because their people enjoy doing great things together.

Index